What They Taught Me is a beautifully engaging guide on how to learn from the wisdom of those who have traveled the path before us. In a time where many of us are longing for deeper and more meaningful connections, this book will help you realize that it's still possible. Kelsey Chapman's storytelling and applicable steps will help you realize the value and power of mentorship.

—**Morgan Harper Nichols** | poet and artist

Kelsey's journey with the mentors in her life shows us that eventually as we grow and expand, we all become the mentors at one point. This book is a refreshing and healing reminder of the hard and the beautiful that shapes our becoming into the people God has orchestrated us to become. Being able to walk through and with Kelsey's healing and her pain was the beautiful remembering of the connectedness we have as women that is often threatened. Kelsey's words remind us that there is healing in togetherness and allows us the graceful permission to reflect on the "what they taught me lessons" from our own lives and how they shaped who we are today.

—**Arielle Estoria** | poet, author, speaker

In *What They Taught Me*, Kelsey speaks with honesty and vulnerability, something we all benefit from when it comes to sitting at the feet of others who have something to teach us. Her insight and wisdom woven through each page prove to be a rich blessing for anyone ready to live a life of wholeness, purpose, and joy.

—**Tiffany Bluhm** | author of *She Dreams* and cohost of the *Why Tho* podcast

Kelsey is one of the most generous women I have ever met. She oozes wisdom and leadership, a̶ ̶ ̶ ̶ ̶ ̶ ̶ ̶ ̶ ̶ ̶ ̶ ̶ ̶ ̶ ̶ ̶ ̶d worthy of investment. *What They 1̶* ̶ ̶ ̶ ̶ ̶ ̶ ̶ ̶ ̶ ̶ ̶ ̶ ̶ ̶ ̶ ̶ ̶ ̶ ̶ι on the vil- lage that raises us—the pe̶ ̶ ̶ ̶ ̶ ̶ ̶ ̶ ̶ ̶ ̶ ̶ ̶ ̶ ̶ ̶ ̶ ̶ ̶h difficulty, who show up to lift us up, and who teach us to give to others as they have given to us. Mentorship often lacks clarity and boundaries, directives and care, but Kelsey clarifies practical steps, wisdom for relating, and the right balance of personal connection and excellence necessary to seek mentorship—and to provide it as well. I want to give a copy of this to every young woman in my life, and you will absolutely be encouraged to do the same.

—**Ashley Abercrombie** | author of *Rise of the Truth Teller*, speaker and host of the *Why Tho* podcast

Kelsey is a mentor for a new generation of young women craving both success and impact. *What They Taught Me* is a must-have resource and inspirational guide to *not* pursuing your dreams all by yourself. It's a must-read for entrepreneurs, grads, and anyone ready to turn their dreams into reality.

—**Anne Samoilov** | podcast host, business strategist, author

One of my favorite quotes ever is this: "If your actions inspire others to dream more, learn more, do more, and become more, you are a leader" (John Quincy Adams). Most people wonder if they even are capable of mentoring, but the reality is we all do in some shape, form, or fashion. Whether you are a reluctant or ecstatic mentor, within *What They Taught Me*, you'll see Kelsey dive deep into this thought of being a leader/mentor with intentionality and consideration for others. It's a book I personally will underline, highlight, and return to often. Love it!

—**Candace Payne** | author, speaker, joy evangelist

WHAT THEY TAUGHT ME

KELSEY CHAPMAN

HARVEST HOUSE PUBLISHERS
EUGENE, OREGON

Published in association with literary agent Tawny Johnson of Illuminate Literary Agency www.illuminateliterary.com

Cover by Faceout Studio

Cover photo © KNST RT STUDIO / Shutterstock

For bulk, special sales, or ministry purchases, please call 1-800-547-8979. Email: Customerservice@hhpbooks.com

What They Taught Me

Copyright © 2020 by Kelsey Chapman
Published by Harvest House Publishers
Eugene, Oregon 97408
www.harvesthousepublishers.com

ISBN 978-0-7369-8062-3 (pbk)
ISBN 978-0-7369-8063-0 (eBook)

Library of Congress Cataloging-in-Publication Data

Names: Chapman, Kelsey, author.
Title: What they taught me : recognizing the mentors who will take you from
    dream to done / Kelsey Chapman.
Description: Eugene, Oregon : Harvest House Publishers, 2020. | Summary:
    "Kelsey Chapman knows what it's like when God brings the right people
    into her path to guide her through difficult seasons personally and
    professionally. Reinvent your concept of mentorship and gain the tools
    you need to invest in the lives of other women"-- Provided by publisher.
Identifiers: LCCN 2020029050 (print) | LCCN 2020029051 (ebook) | ISBN | 9780736980623
    (trade paperback) | ISBN 9780736980630 (ebook)
Subjects: LCSH: Christian women--Religious life. | Mentoring--Religious
    aspects--Christianity. | Female friendship--Religious
    aspects--Christianity.
Classification: LCC BV4527 .C478 2020 (print) | LCC BV4527 (ebook) | DDC
    248.8/43--dc23
LC record available at https://lccn.loc.gov/2020029050
LC ebook record available at https://lccn.loc.gov/2020029051

Printed in the United States of America

20 21 22 23 24 25 26 27 28 / BP-CD / 10 9 8 7 6 5 4 3 2 1

To my mom—
Thank you for being the best role model I could ask for.
And at the same time,
thank you for allowing space for other women to step in
so I could double up on wisdom.
That is the real lesson here.

To my mentors—
Thank you for so generously investing in me,
for passing along the wisdom you gained the long and hard way,
and for allowing me to shortcut the distance to a full and free life
because of your willingness to open up yourselves to me.

And to my Young Life girls—
Thank you for entrusting the most sacred places of your lives to me.
I'm forever changed because of each of you.
Thank you for showing me how to love sacrificially.

To My Parents

Before I go on to honor the women who have taught me as mentors in the chapters to come, I want to begin by honoring my parents. Without their limitless belief in me, I would not be who I am today.

Mom and Dad, thank you for believing in me and continuously reminding me that it's not *the sky's the limit*; it's more like *there are no limits*. Thank you for teaching me to believe I can do anything.

Dad, you championed me as a daughter could only hope her daddy would. You taught me how to work hard and have fun along the way. Our 4,672 nights watching *101 Dalmatians* were probably not the most fun for you, especially before smartphones were invented, but your constant presence and love in my life have never gone unnoticed.

Mom, my greatest gift is that you are my mother. Because of you, I am who I am today. You taught me how to achieve my dreams, showing me what it means to be a strong, powerful woman with no dream too big. You showed me how to be a woman with a drive and passion that can be funneled into a career she loves. Thank you for showing me that I am capable. By seeing you rise to the top in your career, even amid major setbacks, you've shown me I can too.

At the same time, thank you for never presuming to have it all figured out. Thank you for creating space for other women to step in as guides for me. Thank you for never instilling in me the belief that moms are the only women who can invest in the next generation. When I step into motherhood myself in the years to come, you will have already helped take the pressure off; I'll know other women will come alongside my daughter and help instill wisdom in her at just the right time. And I hope to parent her with the openhandedness with which you have parented me.

Thank you for never competing with my mentors because you understood what parenting with open arms looks like. You understood that other women speaking into my life didn't detract from your success as a mother but created an environment for me to learn, grow, and thrive. And while there have been seasons where we both felt that you weren't getting it right and these other women were playing a larger role than you, we were wrong; no one has played a larger role in my life than you. You were and are just the mother I needed.

Lastly, thank you for teaching me that there is always room for healing. You and I have been on a quest toward healing for the better part of our lives. We weren't dealt the easiest cards, and it's taken an incredible amount of work to get here, but you've shown me that healing is possible.

Contents

INTRODUCTION

You know the phrase *It takes a village*? Well, it took a village to raise me into the woman I am today. I'm fortunate to have had more than one woman notice me, come alongside me, and say, "You don't have to do this alone."

Those moments when we're scared about what's next? Those moments when we don't know which path to take? I wasn't alone in those moments. When each season of life invited me into new discoveries, new concerns, new relationships, and new understandings of who I was, I had a guide with me every step of the way.

This book is a love letter to the women who guided me. And it's a love letter to you as you do your own discovering and understanding in whatever season you find yourself.

Through this love letter, I hope not only to teach and encourage you but inspire and shed light on the potential that lies within you and women around you. I wish I could teach you all the things—but there are not enough pages in this book. Yet I hope you'll see my passion for mentorship and that at the very core of my being is the belief that women are unstoppable when we support one another.

I hope you'll learn that it's okay to ask for help. Going at it alone is not a badge of honor—it's really a badge of stubbornness. It might feel good in the moment to be on your own, but life in isolation is not sustainable. We were made to be in relationship. We need one another. So find your village. Find your mentors. Wherever you are on your journey, seek women who are ahead of you on the road and are willing to give you directions. And be willing to ask for them!

Once you have your road map, don't keep it to yourself. Share generously. Look in the rearview mirror and find women a few steps behind you—women who could benefit from the wisdom you've learned or earned. No matter how far you are on the journey, you have something to offer others.

> Mentors are ready to invest in you. And you're capable of being a mentor to someone else.

It's never too late or too soon to start pouring into those around you. Because of the women in this book who patiently loved and championed me along the way, I began mentoring younger women when I was just 19 years old. As you can imagine, I still had a lot to learn myself at that point. But you'll be amazed to see what can happen when your heart is willing and when you trust that the kinks will work themselves out along the way.

Before we dive in, you need to know my story starts out a little rocky. My family, like most, has been no stranger to pain; we've experienced divorce, heartache, and loss, and maybe these types of pain have knocked at *your* door too. As a family of three, we did our best to navigate all this, and my parents made the most of the skills they had in their tool belts. But a village of women stepped up and stepped in, teaching me how to grow through the pain. From them, I learned lessons I might not have picked up otherwise. I learned to face pain head-on. I learned to walk forward in freedom. I learned to invest time in people. And because mentors invested so generously in my life, I learned the gift of investing in others.

My story contains one instance after another of God bringing just the right people to guide me through each season of life. No one woman featured in this book had it all together—just as you and I don't—but each woman was willing to share what she could. I had no expectation that any of them would provide the answers to all my problems or questions. I simply recognized one thing I admired about each of them and asked them to share it with me.

If you're not sure you have time to mentor in an already busy schedule, if you don't feel equipped to mentor, or if you're not sure why mentorship even matters, then keep reading because I'm here to show you how mentorship can take shape in your life. Think of me as your mentorship mentor!

And here's a challenge as you get started: Don't read this book alone! At the end of each chapter, you'll see a list of questions for discussion and reflection, followed by a tangible action step you can take with you into your week. Yes, you can work through these questions on your own, taking time to reflect on them in a separate journal. But your time will be so much richer if it's shared. Enlist a friend or a small group to read this book alongside you, using these questions as prompts to guide your discussion, perhaps once a week. The impact is always bigger when we grow alongside and learn from each other, and sharing this book with a friend or a group is a great way to get the most out of the experience.

As you look forward to investing in other women, you might

> God does tremendous work with a willing heart, and He works out the kinks along the way.

find there are days when you feel discouraged, ready to give up, or as though everyone else is farther down the path toward mentorship than you are. Do not be discouraged! We all wonder if we're unqualified or incapable sometimes. But our shortcomings don't define us, and they don't dictate our future. The fact that God has put this desire in your heart is enough for you to claim the truth that now is the time to start! You are on your way. This journey is one that will lead you toward more beauty, more growth, and more of God's heart. You're at the exact right place to start. Let's get going!

MENTORS LEAN IN...
EVEN WHEN IT HURTS

ONE

Lynell

Of all the women who could have stepped in and played a role in my formation as an adult, Lynell was perhaps the most unlikely. She was never meant to love me. But God knew what He was up to when He wove our stories together.

Lynell is the mother of my oldest and dearest friends, Liala and Emily, and even when I walk up to her glass-paneled front door today, I'm home. After three decades, her house is the one fixture from my childhood that hasn't changed.

Her oldest daughter, Liala, and I met in preschool. We became fast friends and lived two streets apart. We spent summers outside playing with Polly Pockets, pulling each other's hair, and fighting like sisters. We tagged along with each other's families on holidays and vacations, and I was often referred to as her parents' third daughter. Because I was an only child, membership with this duo of sisters and their family felt like all my Olsen twin movie dreams come true.

However ideal this arrangement was for us kids, though, our parents couldn't have felt the same. After a decade of being as close as sisters, as Liala and I were proclaiming our forever friendship, my dad thought it would be funny to casually let us in on the family secret: He and Lynell, Liala's mother, had dated in college.

This bit of information could have been awkward or embarrassing—we were teenagers, after all—but we thought it was the coolest thing ever. This news only strengthened the narrative that we were totally destined to be BFFs. Somehow those two things just had to be correlated, and we had the most unique story of friendship to ever grace God's green earth! The stars had aligned, and here we were, best friends who not only felt like sisters but actually could have been sisters.

I know, this was a little dramatic, but you remember what it was like to be 13—*everything* is a big deal. From our icy roll-on eyeshadow to the latest screen name update on AIM (beachblondie126 for the win) to the new cute boy roaming the halls at school, making a big deal of things was what we did.

Little did we know that Lynell was about to throw us another curveball.

When we brought up her dating history later in the day, at first she looked shocked; it seems there had been some unspoken agreement between our parents to leave the past in the past. Yet my dad had just opened Pandora's box. As Lynell recovered from the surprise, though, she said, "Well, if he opened *that* can of worms, I'll tell you right here that we were engaged."

Engaged! Talk about the unexpected. In our teenage minds, this made our story even cooler. Liala and I loved nothing more than to tell people her mom and my dad were once engaged, as if it solidified our bond.

But it can't have been easy for Lynell to hear that story told over and over. And at 13, we didn't consider that our favorite story had come at a cost. That engagement ended with heartbreak, and Lynell had to sit with the pain before the healing came (which it did—she married an amazing man). Then ten years after the fact, a little blond-haired girl, the daughter of her former fiancé, walked into her life in the form of her own daughter's new best friend. I must have been a constant reminder of her painful past.

As with many childhood friendships, there were sleepovers, drop-offs, and phone calls between parents. Our parents couldn't just ignore one another, especially since our families lived in the same neighborhood. They could have chosen to shut down our friendship, but instead, they chose to face the inconvenience of it, putting aside their pride to let something beautiful blossom between their daughters. This paved the way for Liala's family to become a second family to me, a family that loved me unselfishly despite their past hardships.

One thing I know for sure is that she never expected her path to continue crossing with my dad's world on a regular basis. But because these two little girls were now attached at the hip, she chose to make peace with a not-so-glamorous past. Lynell welcomed me into her family, displaying deep emotional maturity. How would you feel welcoming the daughter of your ex-fiancé into your family and being reminded of your heartbreak on a daily basis? I can imagine that my first inclination would probably not be to treat my ex-fiancé's daughter like my own. Thank goodness for Lynell. She cast off any lingering bitterness in order to model radical action; she loved me despite the fact that I was a constant reminder of her pain. By doing this, by backing up her words with action, and by not allowing bitterness and pain to overtake her, Lynell taught me how to love unconditionally.

It's easy to hold on to feelings of bitterness. It's easy to scorn people who have hurt us and left us with no resolution. I know I certainly wouldn't want to find myself at a playdate with a past love whom I now call Voldemort (jokingly, kind of). But Lynell showed me it's hard to hate people up close, and that it's really tough on everyone to hold on to bad feelings. As the pain begins to dull, then, we're able to see people's humanity in the little day-to-day moments, like weekend drop-offs for sleepovers.

> It's hard to hate people up close.

While it wouldn't have been appropriate to hold the hurts from her relationship with my dad over my head, Lynell didn't have to foster the friendship blossoming between me and Liala. And she *certainly* didn't have to nurture and love me as if I were her own. But Lynell embodied grace. She loved me from the get-go without treating me any differently from the way she would treat any other classmate Liala may have brought into her family's lives. Lynell has consistently shown me, even into adulthood, what it looks like to love when it hurts.

Loving Through the Pain

Not only did Lynell model this grace in the form of loving me to begin with, but she did so even when I was the one causing her pain. A few years back, we talked about a time when, as a teenager, I deeply hurt Liala. My regret about that had lingered with me for years, and I'd had the chance to bring it up and apologize to Liala a few months prior. But I hadn't yet discussed it with Lynell.

The moment for which I was apologizing happened during my "baby Christian" years, perhaps better called my "Bible thumping" years. Leaning into my newfound faith was everything my soul needed. My expression of that faith, though, wasn't what the world needed. I was overzealous, lacking in kindness and compassion. I projected my newfound life principles onto anyone within breathing distance, and judgment was the name of the game. I hadn't yet grasped the kindness of God, and my zeal left broken relationships in my wake. I was clueless as to how to walk out my beliefs in a tactful and noncritical way.

Friendship fumbles marked that season of my life. And on one particular day, I left a long note on Liala's car explaining that we couldn't live together during college because we weren't on the same page. To that note I attached "God's Love Letter"—a cheesy Christian pamphlet. Essentially, I left a friendship breakup letter paired with a Scripture handout on my friend's car.

And Lynell forgave me. I'd hurt her daughter, and she kept loving me. In those years—and particularly on that day—I wasn't just a reminder of her painful past, but a person causing her fresh pain.

So much time has unfolded since then, and Lynell has become more and more of a friend. Even now I can almost feel the two chairs we always sit in to talk or the breeze on my face as we sit on her porch. As much as her home was a fixture in my childhood, it is now a fixture in my adulthood.

On the particular day we sat to discuss this painful season, we sat in these exact two chairs. As usual, the floor was open to discuss anything and everything. I knew it was finally time to apologize to Lynell for how I treated Liala. I knew I had acted a lot more like a Pharisee than a loving follower of Jesus.

"Oh, yes, I was mad at you," she said.

"But you still loved me like your own!"

She smiled at me. "Kelsey, you could have gone totally off the deep end, embracing the party-hard lifestyle of your peers. Instead, you became deeply committed to your faith. While your zeal for your beliefs caused my family pain, I also knew it was saving you. It was what you needed to live a healthy life."

I still regret how I handled my faith in my teen years. I regret how this family, every member so special to me, received the brunt of my judgment. I regret how I misrepresented God as being condemning and without grace instead of grace-filled. But I will never forget how, through that time, Lynell offered *me* unmerited grace.

Another beautiful part of our story is that my grandmother was a mentor to Lynell. Just as Lynell took me under her wing, my grandmother took Lynell under hers. It's not a coincidence that my grandmother played a huge role in Lynell's life and Lynell in mine. It's beautiful to see this legacy of relational investment between our families, first by my grandmother and then by Lynell. In a way, it feels like destiny.

Lynell loved me when I was difficult to love. When I was judgmental, she welcomed me into her home. When I was scared, she left the door unlocked for me to come inside at all hours of the night. When I was sad, she offered me cookie dough and an armchair to watch Jimmy Fallon reruns. When I was figuring out my faith, she offered me grace to explore different beliefs, knowing that would be what ignited my soul. She loved me when my actions hurt her. And when I was first given the role of *mentor* in a formal capacity, I looked back to her example.

Stepping Up

When I was just 19, I inherited a batch of wild 14-year-olds through Young Life, a parachurch ministry to high schoolers who wouldn't typically be interested in attending a local church youth group. Young Life played a significant, stabilizing role for me during my tremendously rocky high school years. Upon entering college, I was eager to go through their leadership training so I could give back to young women in the same way older women had invested in me.

I was a few months into the training when one of the leaders at my alma mater quit. It was a bit premature for me to tackle a mentorship role, but this felt like one of those divine moments when I knew it was my time to step up to the plate. I had a sense that these specific girls were *my* girls and that my role as their leader would give me the opportunity to extend love and care to young women in the same way Lynell had extended love and care to me, even when it was difficult. I also knew I was in for a wild ride—and, boy, did I have a lot to learn!

But I was sold on this little girl gang from the get-go. I remember driving in my car, beaming from ear to ear, filled with hope and excitement for what could play out in the years to come. Of course, I didn't even think to imagine the hard seasons we would navigate. And it wasn't too long before I had my own taste of learning to love when it hurts.

The beauty of my role in these girls' lives was that I hovered somewhere between the roles of sister, friend, and second mom. I received the transparency a friend would receive, the directness a sister might encounter, and the harsh words a mother often absorbs. And very early on, I received all three. One of my girls plunked down in front of me and dove into a diatribe about why one of my family members was going to hell. I believe the lead-in to the conversation was, "How do you feel about [so-and-so] going to hell?"

My facial expressions and body language probably reflected my shock at her lack of tact. But the shock was quickly drowned in a wave of compassion. This was the only lens through which this girl knew to view the world. And it wasn't too long before this conversation that I had been the one delivering harsh blows of judgment across the table toward someone I loved.

I saw myself in her shoes, figuring out her beliefs, wrestling with the big questions of faith, and riding the tension between judgment and the kindness of God. I saw myself in her, and I knew I had an opportunity. My job wasn't to teach her exactly what to believe but to guide her as she navigated her own process—and to hopefully show her that painful questions should be asked with gentleness and compassion.

Moment after moment like this reminded me of Lynell's grace as she loved me through my own not-so-grace-filled moments. She acted as a guide as I arrived at my own values and beliefs, only rarely stepping in and exerting her opinion if needed to preserve my well-being. The beauty of an effective mentor is that they're there for the good, the bad, and the ugly moments—not only for the easy.

Leaning In

The roles of mentor and mentee both come with their fair share of heartache. All relationships can have tough times, and mentoring relationships can have particularly high peaks and particularly low valleys. It's easy to lean in when togetherness is fun—summer nights with my ragtag group of girls are some of my favorite mentoring memories. But the hard moments—the ones that come down to loving, listening, and walking alongside one another even when it's hard to lean in and love, *especially* when it's hard to love—are the moments that build trust and connection that last a lifetime. Who wants a mentor who bails when things get tough?

Certainly, leaving would be the easier choice in some situations. Having lived through hard chapters in both the roles of mentor and mentee, I understand the temptation to give up and run for the hills. But if we truly want to propel each other forward through our mentor and mentee relationships, we have to be willing to stick with it even when it hurts. Weathering hard seasons brings a depth, a richness, and an unmatched value to the relationship. Time and time again I've learned the reward for leaning in during the difficult seasons.

> Let's commit to leaning in when it hurts, to loving our people with longevity.

So my challenge to you and to me is this: Let's commit to leaning in when it hurts, to loving our people with longevity. Ask yourself if you're willing to show up time and time again, both in the good times and in the hard times, to show what unconditional love looks like.

If I've learned anything from my relationship with Lynell, it's that true mentors lean in when it hurts. She could have taken five enormous steps back when I showed up, but instead, she stepped toward me with arms opened wide, embracing me and everything I brought to the table. She became a shoulder to cry on, an ear to listen, and the person who still makes my day all these years later when she yells up to Liala and Emily, "Girls, your sister is here! Come downstairs!"

—— Questions for Reflection and Discussion ——

1. True mentors don't run away from pain; they lean in. What does "leaning in" look like to you? What thoughts, feelings, or emotions surface when you

read this phrase? Can you think of someone who has loved you at your worst? How does that experience encourage you to stick with it when a mentoring relationship grows painful?

2. Mentorship can be uncomfortable. What are some places of discomfort or potential pain points in your own life as a mentor? Can you turn some of them into a mentoring conversation, redeeming them? If so, how?

3. Evaluate your progress when it comes to leaning in through hard times. Are you doing well in this area? In what ways can you improve? With whom have you avoided the tough questions and conversations?

4. Celebrate your people. Make a list of three women whose lives shaped yours in a positive way. Jot down three one-word attributes of each one of these mentors. How were those attributes lived out in their lives? How can you cultivate these attributes in your own life?

· · · · ·

Action Step: This week, schedule coffee with someone you know who's going through a hard time. Lean in and really listen. Embrace what they're bringing to the table, even if it's painful. Be present and offer permission for them to be vulnerable by being vulnerable yourself about your own experience.

MENTORS PLAY
THE LONG GAME

Michelle

For as far back as I can remember, I was unable to sleep alone at night.

When I was a little girl, I slept right smack-dab between my parents in their bed. After their divorce, the co-sleeping continued. I slept with my mom—even throughout my high school years—and at my dad's house, I couldn't bear to be across the hall from him in my own bedroom. But because it would be a tad bit weird for his daughter to sleep in his bed with him, Dad purchased an inflatable twin mattress to keep under his bed and slide out at night. ("Mattress" is generous—it was more like a pool float.) I fell asleep every single night holding his hand, still terrified of the dark but with a little more peace than I would have had sleeping in my own room.

This worked well (for me, not for him) until he remarried. Understandably, my little air mattress situation was not going to work for him and his new wife. I mean, I can't blame them for that one; it's not exactly any newlyweds' dream to have an 11-year-old sleeping on the floor of their bedroom.

They started the grueling process of setting a timer to tell me how long I had to stay in my room, 30 minutes longer each night. I played by the rules, and eventually I wasn't in their bedroom at all. But I developed the bad habit of staying awake until daylight. That's when I finally felt safe enough to sleep alone; I had decided intruders don't usually break in once it's not dark.

Where did such a strong terror of the night originate? You might think a specific incident or trauma spiraled me into years of clinging to the last moments of daylight. But no single moment catapulted me into this level of heightened fear. My parents were baffled by my anxieties, but they also recognized that I needed help, so they always made plenty of room for others to step in and play a supporting role.

At first, this intervention took the form of a counselor. But years passed with little to no progress, and my nightly rituals persisted. By high school, I needed to walk down to my best friend Liala's house on school nights just so I could get a good night's sleep (Lynell's graciousness again on display).

One person recognized the role this fear was playing in my life—my Aunt Michelle.

Going to War

After hearing about my struggles for a long time, and after much prayer behind the scenes, Aunt Michelle stepped in with a game plan. She knew the real root of my fears and recognized them for what they were: spiritual warfare. And she gave me the tactical tools to fight back. In doing so, she enabled me to overcome one of the most challenging parts of my life.

Modeling an intimate connectedness with God, Aunt Michelle taught me to take authority over my fear through prayer. She reminded me that I could pray "on every occasion" (Ephesians 6:18). She showed me how Jesus Himself encouraged us to "keep on asking," promising that we would receive what we needed (Matthew 7:7). I learned that my prayers were more like a conversation and that God was never distant—not even as far as the room across the hall. If I cried, if I whispered, if I just breathed His name, God was always with me.

Aunt Michelle also gave me Bible verses to repeat when I was afraid. In moments of nighttime paralysis, I'd recite psalms I'd memorized just to get through those debilitating hours.

> He will cover you with his feathers. He will shelter you with his wings. His faithful promises are your armor and protection (Psalm 91:4).

> When I am afraid, I will put my trust in you (Psalm 56:3).

> You are my hiding place; you protect me from trouble. You surround me with songs of victory (Psalm 32:7).

And on the hardest nights, when I felt like I could never make it through to morning, Aunt Michelle would listen. She always took my tearful phone calls when I didn't have anyone's bed to crawl into. She never gave me a fast fix, but she was with me every step of the way.

I never experienced a moment of breakthrough with angels singing "Alleluia" or a time when the fear completely disappeared. But in equipping me with God's Word, Aunt Michelle

> Aunt Michelle never gave me a fast fix, but she was with me every step of the way.

showed me I had everything I needed to get me through the worst nights. Even when I couldn't sleep, I was empowered by the knowledge that I wasn't alone. Reciting verses as Aunt Michelle taught me reminded me that God lives inside of me and that I could still find rest knowing the responsibility for this fight wasn't solely on my shoulders.

Fear has been the most debilitating issue in my life, and the journey away from fear has been steep. Especially on those exhausting nights when sleep never comes. But I've also experienced the incredible rewards of the nights, however few and far between, when I've been able to overcome the fear and claim the peace and rest I know is mine.

Aunt Michelle could see what I couldn't—that God is the author of true peace. When I thought fear would claim my sleep forever, Aunt Michelle was there pointing me to the answer.

Playing the Long Game

If there is one person we all need in life, it's someone who keeps showing up and pointing us back to the truth of who we are. Most of our loved ones are there for us in different seasons, swooping in when one crisis or another arises. It would be impossible to expect all our people to rally for us in every moment. But occasionally someone shows up at seemingly all the crucial times and impacts us deeply, leaving us eternally grateful. We all need someone who shows up and *keeps* showing up. Aunt Michelle showed up for me in a moment when I was ready to give up—and she kept showing up.

By overcoming the fear that kept me paralyzed at night, I was able to grow stronger in other areas of my life as well. As I conquered my fear and thankfully settled into healthier patterns of sleep, I had the energy to chase my business dreams and invest in those around me. Working through my fear has changed me, and now I am lucky to teach and empower women around the world to break through the fears and doubts that are holding them back from their dreams. I get to stand in the gap and help these women believe for freedom and a life they love. My fear could have stolen so much from me, and I needed help to fight it. The same goes for you. Maybe your hardship isn't fear. Maybe it's something like anger or shame. But one thing I know for sure is that we're not meant to fight alone. Sometimes we need someone to fight alongside us in the seemingly basic battles of life so we can be strong enough for the bigger battles ahead.

Aunt Michelle modeled for me how I can really be there for those I mentor, not only in the mountaintop moments but also through the inevitable valleys. So when the opportunity came for me to show the same level of commitment for someone I mentored, I was ready to play the long game and love fiercely—through both the good and the bad.

A few years back, a beautiful friend and mentee of mine radically encountered God, and she went on to ministry school to pursue a career on the mission field. Everything was great—at first. But a year into school, she fell into the deepest, darkest depression I had ever encountered and was simultaneously struggling through intense spiritual warfare. She was trying her best to overcome this in the ways she knew how, but depression takes and takes until there's nothing left.

I was ready to dive in headfirst with her, even willing to fly home. But I couldn't—she shut me out, rarely answering my calls. Although I had been cheering her on for the better part of six years at that point, I couldn't support her the way I wished I could. To say it was hard to watch my friend struggle through this battle is an understatement. I felt completely helpless.

So I waited.

And waited.

I knew she wouldn't remain in this state forever. Nope, she had a destiny of joy, fullness, and freedom, and I wasn't going to stop believing in that for her. I was willing to wait it out and pray it out. I was in it for the long haul, and that meant seeing her through the messy middle of her journey. That required patience, but I wasn't in a rush. My job was just to support her in whatever way she would allow.

The times in your mentoring journey where your support is silent can be some of the most crucial and powerful in your mentoring relationship. If the person you're mentoring is in a season of pushing people away, unable to receive support, your mentorship may look different. It may look like standing in prayer or sending notes of encouragement—*I'm here when you're ready. I'm not going anywhere.* Silence and waiting do not mean inactivity. Your consistency will make all the difference when the friend you're mentoring is ready to let you in again.

I so desperately wanted to rescue this sister of mine, but I just had to pray and wait. And after a few years, the darkness started to make way for the light. She returned to her old self, and slowly but surely I saw that old spark and passion return to her—this time with a depth that only comes through perseverance.

Recently, I sat across from her as she told me about the ways she's recognized that God has carried her over the last year, even when He felt absent. We wept together over how she's returning to the school where all the hard stuff started. She's confident that this deeply scary and painful season is being redeemed and brought full circle. I encouraged her, and I told her that I've always believed in her and I'm beyond excited for the next season ahead of her.

As we sat together, I couldn't help but think of Aunt Michelle, how she trusted the process even when it meant patiently waiting on me to course correct if I took a wrong turn; the way she knew in her heart that I would. Just as I was able to do for the friend in front of me, she never worried, knowing that if she played the long game with me, it would all work out in time.

When I was in high school, I had early dismissal from school on Thursdays, and Aunt Michelle and I made this time our window to meet. Once the bell rang, I headed straight to her house to enjoy a simple lunch together before my lifeguarding shift. Sometimes it was just a lunch packed with great conversation, sometimes it was a discussion about how to navigate teenage or family drama, and other times it was a quick dive into the Bible or something she'd read and thought would be helpful and pertinent to my life.

I didn't need Aunt Michelle to offer a momentous piece of wisdom that changed my life every Thursday. I needed her to show up. Consistency always trumps fancy words or mind-blowing messages. When we get to the end of our lives, we won't remember the sermons or the keynotes people shared with us; the little moments we spent together will have made the biggest impact. And those small moments are what I cherish from my time with my Aunt Michelle. I remember the way I felt when I was with her—safe, seen, and accepted. That's what we're all looking for.

> I didn't need a momentous piece of wisdom that changed my life.
> I needed her to show up.

So how will you show up? Will you muster all that you have and pretend you have it all together? Or will you present yourself—struggles and all—and offer the experience and support you have to give? I believe that, most times, you don't have to "muster up" something to offer someone; you simply have to give out of the overflow of what's already there.

Recently, when my husband's travel schedule amped up again, Aunt Michelle was the first person to check in with me. She hadn't forgotten the anguish of those sleepless years, and it was sweet of her to recognize that while this was an exciting new season of our life, it would also hit a sensitive spot for me. She looked at me across the table during breakfast and said, "I know this is going to be hard. What's your game plan?"

She wasn't wrong. I had been worrying about myself amid a season of celebrating.

All these years later, she just knew. And her intentional love prompted her to initiate a conversation that might mean revisiting the same exhausting topic we'd come back to year after year. But she was willing. Aunt Michelle has never quit being there for me. Even after three decades, she's still praying over a problem that ultimately is not hers and reminding me of the power of investing in your people with consistency and longevity.

—— Questions for Discussion and Reflection ——

1. Who played a pivotal role in your early faith journey?

2. Who has been a consistent presence in your life?

3. Who has rallied for you in the hardest parts of your life? Have you allowed those people to walk with you in the darkest places, to guide you? Or have you always tried to walk through them alone?

4. Brainstorm some places in your world where you might find a mentor who can play this supportive role. Remember, though, that this person may reveal themselves over time.

5. If you removed the pressure of needing to have all the answers, do you feel like you could show up for someone consistently? What would that look like for you?

• • • • •

Action Step: This week, reach out to someone who has chosen to walk the road with you through a dark season and thank them. That could look like taking some time to sit down and handwrite a thoughtful letter to mail to them. It could look like taking this person out to lunch if you still live in the same area and updating them on how their intentionality from that season has impacted where you're at today. This brings full circle the unstoppable power of coming alongside one another and lifting each other up so that we are empowered and encouraged to continue championing generations that come after us.

MENTORS INVEST WITHOUT A GUARANTEED RETURN

THREE

Emily

My friends and I blazed into Emily's life when we were just 14 years old, all with a heavy mix of sass and insecurity. At age 19, Emily must have thought we were the hot mess express. And she was right.

As the self-proclaimed hot stuff of our town, we spent our time bumping down the street to rap music, wearing the latest on-trend tube tops, and hitting the teen clubs during the golden era of T-Pain and Lil Wayne. We were living the life, y'all! Maybe you thought my teenage years were centered more around Bible studies and Sunday school. Nope. My girl gang was wild, and Emily loved us somethin' fierce.

We met Emily at our local Young Life gathering. Young Life was all the rage on Monday nights at my high school. The word on the street was that we didn't have to be a super Christian, have it all together, or fit into a mold to show up there. Anyone was welcome to come have fun, play games, and talk a little bit about faith.

I wasn't really the youth group kind of kid, but I had been curious about who God really was. So this seemed like a perfect way to ask questions (and meet cute boys) without someone beating me over the head with their Bible.

I didn't know it then, but this ministry was cultivating a space where I could "belong before believing." Or, in my case, belong while trying to work out the nuances of what it meant to follow Jesus.

Emily was assigned to our grade, and she was quickly embraced as the leader of our pack. I knew she cared about me, and that security gave me the comfort to really dig in, ask hard questions, and figure out what I believed.

Even with my small framework of understanding, I had been deeply connected to the idea of God since I was a little girl. Even without reading the Bible, going to church, or knowing much about Jesus at all, I can clearly remember giving my life to Him on a paddleboat at summer camp on a sweltering July day, somewhere around the age of nine. From that point forward, I was looking and longing for someone to show me how to walk out my faith in a tangible way.

Church seemed scary and filled with perfect people with perfect lives—people to whom I couldn't relate. I was scrappy, wild, and far from the mold of what Southern Christianity said I should be. Remember, I was a tube-top-wearin', teen-club-dancin', rap-music-listenin' kind of gal. I was way more interested in watching MTV's *Road Rules* than in memorizing Scripture. In my gut I knew there had to be Christians out there like me. And as I searched for them, my intrigue with God and what He was all about didn't fade.

Right around that time, at *the* most pivotal age of my life, Emily entered the scene.

Letting Me Be Me

Emily gave me permission to thrive in my own skin and stay true to who I was while pursuing my faith. She demonstrated that Christianity wasn't a behavioral modification program; I could show up as my messy and truest self. She didn't ask me to be someone I wasn't, showing me that Jesus doesn't ask that of us either. And that grace was the greatest gift I could have asked for in a mentor, especially in those delicate, early years of my faith.

Emily also didn't expect me to get it all together overnight. She walked with me day after day, month after month, year after year— through the boyfriend drama and the raging hormones that mark the teenage years. At just 19, she was modeling the art of investing without an immediate return, trusting that her investment would pay off. And I'm so glad she did, because not only did her example change my life, but it taught me how to mentor from a place of grace and generosity. Emily didn't try to control the outcome of her investment of time and energy. Instead, she trusted that we would bloom into something beautiful.

When Emily met my friends and me, she didn't know us at all. We could have been the rottenest 14-year-olds to ever exist on planet Earth (and we certainly were at times). She had no reason to step in and care for us other than her desire to invest in and impact women coming behind her. Emily proved she was going to be there for us no matter what. And she was there, *always*—in the moments when we were acting like angels but also in the moments when we were possessed by teenage angst.

And she *chose* to do this, in college, on nights and weekends when she could have been out painting the town or going on dates. I can appreciate the magnitude of her choice now, but as a 14-year-old, I didn't even think about what she was giving up to spend time with us. My friends and I had no concept of the emotional, financial, and intentional time investment Emily was making to serve us. We just thought it was pretty cool that a college girl wanted to hang out with us. And she didn't just spend time with us at random; she took us to fall and summer camp, had us over to her house with endless supplies of bean dip and cookies, and met us every Tuesday morning over coffee and muffins to catch up on life and talk about Jesus.

To us, each meeting seemed like just another fun hangout. Sure, we understood that sometimes the purpose was to dig deeper into the Bible, and we were fine with that. But the beauty of a mentoring relationship is that it doesn't have to be structured to be meaningful. It was so much more about showing up in the little moments. Emily built trust little by little, building connections with us girls so we could feel safe enough to receive the wisdom she carried.

> A mentoring relationship doesn't have to be structured to be meaningful. It's so much more about showing up in the little moments.

In my relationship with Emily, perfectionism wasn't demanded of me, and grace was always extended. One evening at youth camp, the 15 of us girls walked out the door ready for the country-themed night. We'd turned our tanks into crop tops and strutted our daisy dukes with a flannel tied around our waists. And Emily didn't blink. Now, she may have had a little laugh with the other leaders while taking her girls in barely-there outfits to hear the good news of the gospel. But she never made us feel uncomfortable. She always accepted us just as we were.

This was just what I, what *we*, needed. While in the past I had crumbled under the pressure of who the church said I had to be,

I thrived under the banner of total acceptance. I thrived and ran toward God and the freedom He offered.

If we're honest, don't we all thrive when we are fully accepted, just as we are? People *crave* acceptance, and giving it works! Meeting people where they are and letting them experience acceptance and love over judgment is always the right choice. We aren't called to approach people with a laundry list of criteria they have to meet before they're welcomed into the fold. What I've learned, and what I've found to be the most deeply impactful in my own experience, is that we're called to love. Period. And this assignment never places us in the judge's seat.

Emily accepted me without trying to change me. Instead of judging me, she chose to pour into me time and time again even though no obvious fruit was coming from her labor. Investing in someone without a guaranteed return means being present and available from the start and sticking it through in those messy middle phases. It means making the hard choice to show up because you believe that empowering the women coming behind you is the very best thing you can do.

The huge investment Emily made on my Young Life group was completely lost on us. But little by little, everything she sowed into us began to bloom into something bigger. Her patience and intentionality, her sacrificial investment of time, set us on the road to finding ourselves and hammering out our belief systems that would carry us through the years to come.

Five years later, I stepped into the same shoes as Emily, working with an equally rowdy group of high schoolers.

> I committed to loving for the long haul. I couldn't count on seeing the fruits of my labor or knowing how my investment of time would pay off.

Thankfully, as I mentored these gals, I could pull from the lessons she taught me. Following in her footsteps, I quickly learned that as a mentor who was growing deeply attached to these girls, I also had to be committed to loving for the long haul. I couldn't count on seeing the fruits of my labor or knowing how my investment of time would pay off.

Choosing One Another

My first few years were mostly fun and effortless. Thankfully, my girls chose me as much as I chose them. We felt like one big happy family. And then the monstrosity of junior year hit. My little munchkins blossomed into women who were less interested in sleepovers and more interested in ditching me for the latest boy who gave them attention or a party that was all the rage. I remember looking at my girls one day—sweet and snarky teenagers who still enjoyed my company—and then, seemingly the next day, they changed before my eyes. Overnight, they became a bratty force, dead set on the idea that they did *not* need me hanging around.

Annoying? Yes. I remember thinking with my profound martyr complex, *They don't appreciate me and everything I do for them. They don't even care.* The feelings of underappreciation were so bad that I began formulating my escape. I would flee to Australia, where I would spend endless days at the beach and be done with this. I had elaborate ideas for how I could get out of there, and I even had a school picked out for a transfer. This was a real escape plan, not just a daydream.

But in the end, like Emily, I chose not to quit. Mentorship isn't always easy, especially when your mentees are navigating how to process an already difficult season of life. The rainbows and butterflies give way to stormy days, but mentorship means trusting they will come again.

And here's the thing...as a mentor, you *will* give more than you take. You'll have to remind yourself that the return is not immediate. If you can be patient and stick it out, though, the rewards will come over time. When we are able to shift into this perspective, we'll find that the burden lifts and eases the pain that often comes in a nonreciprocal relationship.

This is one of the reasons it's so important to have a mentor even while you're mentoring someone else. If you give and give and give without ever receiving, you'll find yourself ready to give up. If you're going to pour *out* to another person, make sure someone else is pouring *into* you.

And here's the great news: The blessing of mentorship goes both ways. As a mentee, you open yourself to so much wisdom. But as a mentor you also have unique opportunities to learn about yourself. You learn about patience. You learn how to listen with the intent to understand rather than with an already formulated response. You learn how to make someone feel heard instead of preached at. You learn how to make massive amounts of treats on a budget. You learn that despite the time sacrificed with your peers, the most real and satisfying reward is the eternal investment you're making in others.

Even If...

Have you turned down the chance to pour into someone's life because fear told you not to? Have you made excuses for why you can't be a mentor? I get it. I believed so many lies before I pushed them aside and entrusted myself to the task. I was trapped in untruths, asking questions like...

- What if, after all those hours of love and attention, my mentee doesn't value me?

- What if she doesn't love me back?

- What if there are no results to show for my time investment?

- What if I don't have enough time?

- I figured things out with no one pouring into me, so won't others be fine if I don't invest in them?

Do any of those questions sound familiar? While the thoughts behind them are all valid, it's a disservice to let your fears rule your decisions. So try this: Instead of asking *what if,* turn the question into a statement of faith. Change the *what if* to *even if.*

- Even if she doesn't appreciate the hours of love and attention I give, I'll become a better listener and be a more patient friend through the experience.

- Even if she doesn't like me at times, I trust that our paths have come together for a reason.

- Even if there are no results for my time investment, I trust that the seeds planted are dormant, not dead, and they'll spring up at just the right time.

- Even if I don't have much time, I trust that even just a moment can be used to change someone's life, making an hour of my month pouring into others a worth-while investment.

- Even if no one poured into me, I hope to offer her something I didn't have.

Sometimes what we see right in front of us is only a dim reflection of the big picture ahead. You'll spend countless hours with a girl and begin to see her come alive, only to have her fall off the face of the earth and ignore you for two years. (Been there.) You'll tirelessly answer call after call from a mentee, mustering up the best wisdom you've got, only to have her *not* take your advice. (Been there too.)

You will certainly feel weary in moments of mentorship. Giving without an expectation of getting back can't *always* be lifegiving—unless you're a saint. (And if you are a saint, then props to you, and thanks for reading this book!)

You *will* get tired. You *will* have to learn to set boundaries when you realize you overdid it. You *will* reframe your expectations, usually *after* a bout of disappointment. You *will* want to give up—some days. You *will* look at that mentee in front of you and think, *Is this really working? Is this really going anywhere?* There *will* be moments you doubt yourself.

When those feelings threaten to overwhelm you, remember that nothing is ever lost, even though it can all feel lost in a moment. What you've invested matters, and the love you give is a powerful force that never returns void.

—— Questions for Discussion and Reflection ——

1. Has anyone invested in you without strings attached? How does this make you rethink investing in others and what that can or should look like?

2. What would it look like for you to invest in someone without strings attached? What would be difficult about that for you?

3. What are some hesitations you have when it comes to investing in someone? How can you reframe your *what ifs* as *even ifs*?

Action Step: Write out a list of reasons you've hesitated to get more deeply involved in a mentoring relationship. Work on reframing them as *even ifs*, changing those hesitations into affirmations.

What About the Wrong Mentors?

I fully believe in mentorship, and I have significantly benefited from it. I have found that the reward of mentorship is greater than the risk. But I do have to tell you, risk does come with the territory.

Risk comes with any type of relationship, but when you allow someone to speak into your life, it's especially important to be mindful of the risk you're taking. You're allowing someone to not only listen to you but to offer you wisdom and input, and a high level of discernment is necessary. Some mentors will not be the best fit for you.

> Risk comes with any type of relationship, but when you allow someone to speak into your life, it's especially important to be mindful of the risk you're taking.

That's why trial and error is part of the quest for mentors. Finding a mentor can be like dating to find someone compatible; the risk of some missed connections is always worth the reward of finding someone you can relate to.

And the risk of looking for someone who's willing to step in and help you shortcut the hard lessons of life is that a trial might end with error.

One experience of mine illustrates this point well. About midway through college, I had my first experience with a mentor that went sideways. During this period of my life, I was deeply involved at church and heavily invested in a small group of about 20 friends that met each Tuesday. We were led by a young couple in their midthirties. They were charismatic, kind, and insanely hospitable to let this bustling group of college students and young adults into their home each week. This couple was very committed to the group, and my friends and I felt lucky to have not only their guidance but their friendship as well. We trusted them as a team of mentors.

But I had a bit of a problem with this small group. I had a crush on one of the other members, and when I had a crush on someone, I became all kinds of awkward. Normally the life of the party, my usual bubbly self instead became tongue-tied and essentially mute—and not the cute kind of quiet. The awkward kind.

Because of this weird shift in my demeanor, I seemed a bit "off" at the small group meetings, and our leaders pulled me aside to ask me a few questions. I don't blame them for doing this, because I know I wasn't acting like myself.

The conversation started with genuine concern. They wondered if everything was okay or if I needed help with anything. But then our talk took a turn. The wife rehashed her own story, which was one of abuse and molestation as a child. That was definitely a direction I did not expect. And then they told me they thought I, too, had been molested as a child. They believed God wanted them to tell me to "stop hiding."

I had heard about repressed memories in therapy and had ever wondered if I might have them. And in this moment, I thought this must be the case. *Oh no,* I thought. *This must be true.*

As an impressionable young woman who truly trusted these mentors, I began to twist the jitters from a crush into "hiding" from something bigger. I tried to unearth all those suppressed memories and face the "reality" that I was hiding from something darker and more sinister than social anxiety. I became convinced of a reality that didn't exist.

I thought, *God has to be cluing them in, right?* I never imagined that my small-group leader could simply be projecting her story onto me. I accepted that this was my new reality—that I was an abuse survivor suppressing memories that were bound to surface sooner or later. I dreaded what those memories would be.

That night I quietly headed home, mentally unpacking the magnitude of what this revelation meant. My leaders had assigned me a book on abuse they said had helped them, and they scheduled a time to meet later to review what I read.

And this is how *the month of frantically digging* started. I carried that book everywhere. I mulled over thoughts from my childhood constantly, digging for any memory that I might have been blocking so I could begin the healing process. I replayed scenario after scenario in my head, looking for any missed bread crumb of a memory. I dissected every moment that came to mind, trying to determine whether my positive thinking had reframed a tortured event into something less painful.

To say it was an exhausting month would be an understatement. My every waking thought was fixated on this potential memory that I had supposedly blocked out. *How long ago had it been? How old was I? What would unleash when I finally traced back to the moment it happened?*

As I mulled over some of the unsupervised times of my childhood, searching for any semblance of a memory of when someone could have hurt me, I decided it was time to call Aunt Michelle. This would be way too big of a curveball to present to my parents without proof. I didn't want to scare my family, but I had to know. I had some big questions, and I hoped my aunt might have some recollection of odd behavior from me, or that she would know of a situation that would have left me exposed to danger.

Aunt Michelle heard me out, helped me pray through the array of feelings pulsing through me, and asked the simple question, "Could they have been wrong?" She had no recollection of any weird behavior from me, and she had confidence that no telltale signs of abuse had shown up in my childhood.

Having a trusted mentor like Aunt Michelle helped me see through what these other voices were telling me. I doubted if I could trust my small group leaders, and I couldn't trust myself to determine what was reality and what wasn't. Aunt Michelle was the voice of reason who showed me, yet again, the example of what being a mentor is all about. It's not about projecting our experiences on someone else. It's about pointing people toward the truth. If I hadn't had Aunt Michelle, I don't know what would have happened. Would I have believed I had been molested as a child although I most definitely hadn't? Would I have taken the word of my mentors, simply because they were older and, I thought, wiser?

This very painful experience taught me something important: Just because someone is well-intentioned and respected in the community you participate in doesn't mean they're a fit to have total say-so for you. It's easy to be swept up into the idea that every captivating, compelling human should speak into your life—especially in the church. But just because they're captivating and compelling doesn't mean they have total authority over you.

And these are the moments when it's important to have trusted guides to come alongside you. Maybe you haven't kept in touch with them. Maybe it's been years since you last spoke. But we all need those people who have stuck with us through the long haul, to help us discern the next step in the inevitable scary situations. We need to lean heavily on those people to get us through the toughest of seasons.

This was one of the most painful seasons of my faith walk. And it had me wrestling with my lack of surety. All the while, I was still showing up to this small group and seeing those leaders every week. Ultimately, I had to say to them, "Thank you for caring enough to speak up about what you felt about me, but I don't think this happened to me, and I'm going to stop digging."

This was one of those lessons that didn't end well. My Tuesday night group dissolved over this incident, and it was painful. And even through the pain, I knew I was going to miss the voices of these mentors and spending my Tuesday nights on their couch. This situation marked the close of a chapter and the loss of something I deeply valued, yet taught me that not everyone is the right mentor for me or for a particular season.

The pain of a mismatched mentor is real—I know it too well! But we can't let a painful experience dictate our future. Know that even though it might take several attempts to find the right fit, the journey will be worth it in the end. How many great mentoring relationships would I have missed if my story stopped here? If I had thrown in the towel and said, "That was painful and I'm done being hurt. I'm never doing that again"? I promise you, it is absolutely worth continuing in your pursuit of mentorship. Keep going! Don't give up and and don't miss out on the mentors who might change your life forever.

MENTORS
GET COMFORTABLE
WITH PAIN

FOUR

Kay

Do you have people in your life who can't seem to discuss deeper issues? One mention of how you've been feeling depressed and they're trying to get you to laugh with a joke? For some reason or another—often their own inability to deal with discomfort—some people always feel compelled to *keep it light*.

I sure know some of those people. But Kay was different. She cultivated space for those lighter moments filled with laughter and stories from our day-to-day experiences, yet she also left plenty of room to go deep—even when the room filled with that awkward tension that comes from navigating the grittier parts of life. Even during those moments with ugly cries and mascara running down 19-year-old faces on her couch, Kay made emotional space.

I met Kay my freshman year of college. She's got the cutest pixie haircut, she's as warm as they come, and she's the mother of kids just a few years ahead of me. One day during my first semester, I found myself on a couch in her living room. She was hosting a Bible study organized for Young Life leaders-in-training. Each week she opened her home to my group of friends and me so we could learn about one another's stories and dive into a devotional together. It was meant to be a time to bond as leaders, but as much as we loved one another, we loved seeing Kay all the more.

Being at her home was a highlight in our week. We knew we were in the midst of forming lifelong friendships; we envisioned ourselves one day pushing strollers together—or as we called it, "mom walking," with a nod to our future by calling ourselves the "mom five." As we formed those relationships, we were grateful to have an adult figure willing to carve out one night of every single week so she could spend time with us. We had the chance to walk through the "big stuff" with someone who had a little more of life figured out than we did.

When our weekly Bible study came to a close, Kay and I segued into monthly coffee dates (or Diet Coke in Kay's case), continuing our conversations. She and I had walked a strikingly similar path, and I felt such safety in knowing that she understood the depths of my story. I'd had no idea that meeting someone who had walked a similar road could offer relief and rescue from loneliness, but once I discovered it, I knew it would be pivotal for my wholeness and freedom moving forward.

For so long I had felt isolated by my story. Now the story was what drew Kay and me together.

Trying to Escape a Story

Kay's story was quite like my own. As an adolescent, she had navigated the pain of family heartache. As an adult, she'd had to reconcile how her past had shaped her story. She had done the hard work of healing from her pain, and she showed up in my life at just the right time to help me start doing the same. Being a few years ahead of me on this journey, she had already lived the season

I felt I was in. I was able to learn and draw from the wisdom she'd gained, seeing how the wounds of our pasts didn't need to become permanent scars.

Before beginning my own healing journey, I had spent most of my time escaping my pain. Whenever I felt the hurt bubbling up, I booked a fun adventure or filled my calendar with social activities. I'd have two dollars in my bank account and still make room for that quick road trip. I'd scrounge up some airline reward miles from someone to *just get away*.

> The wounds of our past don't need to become permanent scars.

But one day, in the midst of planning one of my adventures, a college sweetheart looked me in the eye and said, "You're at your happiest when you're about to leave on a trip, but I think you're trying to escape your life."

Ouch! Put that way, my fun, bubbly self didn't sound all that healthy. I loved to travel, so I had always interpreted these tendencies to get away as a part of my free-spirited nature. But then he mentioned this whole *escape* thing, and I realized he wasn't wrong. Maybe my adventures were a way to numb myself, to shut down the grief, to quiet any inkling that all might not be well.

After this reality check, I resolved to stop running from what I was facing. But I desperately needed a support system—someone who could go beyond sympathy and extend empathy toward this kind of pain. I needed someone who had lived it. I didn't want to be added to another prayer chain or to be handed more Scriptures to memorize. I'm not dismissing those tactics—remember how the Scripture my aunt gave me to memorize was so helpful? But now I needed practical tips for how to overcome this pain—no casseroles, no awkward group prayers over me, please.

Thankfully, Kay was the pillar I needed. My coffee dates with her soon became conversations where she helped me navigate painful events that had unfolded between my two homes. We built a friendship that naturally allowed me space to process the fear of how my story might affect my future.

> We can use our pain productively, first by working through it for our own healing and then by coming alongside someone else a few years behind us on the journey.

While none of us are strangers to pain—we'll all experience it in some capacity during our lifetime—we can use that pain productively, first by working through it for our own healing and then by coming alongside someone else a few years behind us on the journey. Kay taught me that sharing what we know is a simple but powerful form of aiding someone through the darkest seasons of life.

Not only did Kay help me face and process my pain, but she gave me the courage to consider using my story to help others the same way she used hers to help me. Maybe I could be a beacon of light in other people's darkness, so that those who resonated with my story might not feel so alone.

Safe Havens

I began to share parts of my story in safe spaces in the coming years, and through this newfound vulnerability, I was able to create a safe haven for peers navigating the same family dynamic. In sharing our stories, I felt all of us stepping out of isolation. We took a journey of totally uprooting the weeds that had grown in our hearts—the weeds of limiting beliefs, guardedness, and heartache that prevent us all from moving forward.

Without Kay teaching me how to process my pain, how would

I have been able to show up for others who had a similar story? Without first healing from my own pain, how could I fulfill my dreams and aspirations of pouring into my generation of women? Kay had done the hard work of healing herself, and her hard work paved a path for me to follow suit.

My own healing journey taught me that it's easy to isolate yourself, believing your story alienates you from others. But no matter what you've lived through or the pain you've experienced, your limiting beliefs are probably more similar to others' than you think. No one is a stranger to hardship, and there's no way any of us will make it through this life untouched by pain. Your flavor of trauma might be different from someone else's, but we all share the commonality of hardship. That means we can have compassion when we look to the right and to the left and realize a neighbor is battling her own unique brand of suffering.

That compassion is the best qualification for mentorship. You don't need to have it all together to be a mentor. You don't need to be a mind reader or have a long list of qualifications. You don't even have to put on a smile. You just need to say, "I've been hurting, too, and here's how I got through it."

When we keep our stories in the dark, they grow and control us. Instead of facing our stories head-on, we try to ignore the pain, all the while giving the narrative more space in our minds. We seek to push back all the thoughts about the areas we deem "too messy," and we hold ourselves back. Instead of facing the story, we let it dictate who we are. Only when we bring it out into the light do we have true freedom. And from that place of walking in our own freedom, we're able to extend that gift of freedom to others.

I went through therapy for the better part of the next ten years after meeting Kay, fully committed to cultivating my emotional health. It was tedious, laborious work. Often, I would show up to therapy feeling fine—only to discover that what I'd expected would be an "easy session" ended up being one of the hardest ones. I was shocked at what a big impact seemingly insignificant experiences were having on my adult life.

Wading through the pain points of my life hasn't been easy, but the more I chose to lean in, the more I was able to see the hard work of soul healing pay off. What once was pain I desperately wanted to lock in the basement of my soul—never to be seen again—became my qualification to give others the courage to lean in so that they could overcome the harder parts of their story.

Trust Takes Time

I began to find healing from my past right at the time I began my own journey into mentorship. As I started leading my tribe of amazing young women, I began to realize they had their own woundings they were carrying. When I looked at them, I saw confident smiles. Behind those smiles, though, were the harsh and isolating realities and secret depths of pain. And I'm not talking about minor trials and tribulations. I'm talking about the worst kinds of pain. Divorce. Heartbreak. Loss. Wading through these experiences is hard enough as an adult, but for a teenager, it can be excruciating. Just as I had, they needed someone to tell them they weren't alone in their heartache. They needed someone who had trudged through the same maze and learned the best way through.

As a mentor, building the trust to tackle these topics takes time. It's rare to meet someone who will share their entire story, pain, confusion, and struggles with you without first knowing your intentions toward them. Cautious human beings are aware of how misplaced vulnerability can harm them. You have to set the table of trust by first showing that you're genuine in your care.

And what sets the table for that kind of trust? Our own vulnerability and transparency. Kay's willingness to share her story made me feel safe enough to trust her with the darkest places in my own life. As a result, I made it my mission to apply these same lessons to the relationships I would go on to foster.

Were the painful parts of my story "worth it" so I could lift up others? I don't know. But one thing I do know: Since these parts of my story are never going away, I might as well make the most of them by giving that pain a purpose and using it to serve others, just like Kay did for me.

I'm not the first or last person impacted by events outside her control. But Kay showed me that shared pain is an opportunity to forge a connection and show compassion.

I don't remember a single thing from my Bible study with Kay, but I sure learned from her. How liberating to realize that our impact as a mentor isn't so much about the lessons we directly teach but the stories we tell—stories of our own experiences that might just help others navigate theirs.

Kay used her life to minister to

> As we reach toward the hand extended to us from someone who has walked the same road, we can use that hand to pull ourselves up. And then, once we have navigated our own pain, it's our turn to extend a helping hand to the woman a few steps behind us.

> Shared pain is an opportunity to forge a connection and show compassion.

mine, and she opened the door for me to begin healing from the circumstances I believed would mark my life forever. Today, my unique brand of family heartache doesn't define me. It's a part of my story but not its totality. Because Kay chose to invest in me, care for me, and walk with me, I was able to see the bigger picture of life and truly embrace it for what it is.

One of my favorite Scripture verses is, "They overcame him by the blood of the Lamb and by the word of their testimony" (Revelation 12:11 NKJV). This verse reminds me that our stories, paired with the gospel, allow us to overcome the harder parts of our stories and empower us to excel in the years to come. And *your* story, no matter how many bumps you've had along the way, might just help someone overcome their own darkness. The stories of the women who came before me and their willingness to allow me to learn from them, no matter how imperfect, paved the way for my own freedom.

Thankfully, the mentors in my life have shared both the mountaintops and the valleys of their lives with me. They showed me how I could learn from their stories in order to move forward into the fullness of my destiny. They showed me that true mentorship is about allowing the ones coming behind me to go further than I did. They allowed me to stand on their shoulders so I could push through the ceiling of what held them back. And from their wisdom and guidance, I've been able to navigate some of the hardest seasons with my girls.

Would I wish any of us to have to walk through the painful experiences we face in life? No. Sometimes, even when standing on our mentors' shoulders, we don't reach the ceiling or break through it like we thought we would. Sometimes our pain never ends tied up in a beautiful bow. But God is a God of redemption, and He uses *all* circumstances of our lives for His glory and our good. Our ceiling, and the good and bad parts of our stories, can become the floor for the next woman to stand on so she can go further than we ever did. And for that, the journey is worth it.

—— Questions for Discussion and Reflection ——

1. Can anyone in your life help you navigate those painful parts of your story?

2. How do you think you could best support someone who's navigating the same pain you've experienced? What's the route you took out of the maze of your story, and how could you share it with others?

3. Have you ever avoided sharing your story with someone for fear of being too vulnerable?

• • • • •

Action Step: This week, show intentional vulnerability. Share your story with a friend or neighbor, and then open yourself to hearing hers.

MENTORS ARE CALLED, NOT QUALIFIED

FIVE

Harriet

Harriet was the mother of one of my high school guy friends, who lived down the street from me. All through my teenage years I spent countless nights in Harriet's driveway, hanging out with our group of more than 20 teenagers. I'm sure she made her home the landing place for her children's friend groups because she thought it was better to have us in her driveway than heaven knows where else, and we were there every weekend without fail. I think we girls even fell asleep upstairs in her bonus room on a few occasions.

In college, I became the Young Life leader to her daughter, Laura Grace, so nights in her driveway with my friends turned into evenings in her kitchen eating snacks with a bunch of 14-year-old girls who were now claiming her living room as *their* mainstay.

So many of my most precious memories from the eight years of high school and college were formed at some spot in her home: her driveway, her bonus room, her kitchen table, her living room when she hosted Young Life club. It was one of my favorite places to be on any given weekend. Each time I found myself laughing as we all huddled around Harriet's kitchen counter, I would catch myself thinking, *This is the life I want to create for my own family.*

Something about being at Harriet's house was so comfortable. Her home radiated peace. And don't get me started on her cooking; she always had the *best* food. Really, it was just the center of our little universe, being near all our houses and local haunts. Being at her house made me dream about my own future family and home. Like her, I wanted to create a home with a revolving door of friends and kids who would feel like my space was theirs.

Why Not Ask?

During my second year as a youth leader to Harriet's daughter, I decided I had watched from the sidelines long enough. I wanted to know Harriet's secret. I wanted to know how she created such a lovely space where everyone wanted to be. She wasn't striving for perfection, but in her intentionality she'd cultivated something beautiful, and I loved watching as she continued to do so. I wanted to know the key to creating the life I wanted one day for my own family, so I thought, *Hey, why not ask to meet and chat?* About what, I wasn't sure. But I admired Harriet, and I hoped she would pass down what she'd learned in her years of married life and motherhood.

If it's true that we are the sum of the people with whom we surround ourselves, then it couldn't hurt to add Harriet to my inner circle and learn from the best!

When I asked Harriet to meet me for coffee on a regular basis, I was a bit nervous. Other than admiring the life she'd built, I didn't have an exact reason for getting together, and it seemed like I was stepping outside the typical mold of mentorship by asking someone to pour something so intangible into me. But again, thus far my eagerness to learn from the women a few steps ahead of me had yielded far more reward than pain, so I figured it couldn't hurt to ask.

At first Harriet seemed surprised, most likely not thinking of herself as a formal mentor. She hadn't realized the way she was living her life was something another person would want to emulate. But that was fine with me. I had no concrete expectations of her; I just loved watching her life unfold. I respected that she had a marriage that was connected, friendships that ran deep, and kids who enjoyed her company as we lingered in her kitchen for hours at a time. Lucky for me, she said yes—no longer was she just my friend's mom whom I admired from afar; Harriet was a woman to whom I could turn to discuss life's greatest milestones.

Just as Harriet first questioned whether or not she was "mentor material," we often have so many ideas about what a mentor "should" be. At work, it's the CEO whose career is so admired that every younger woman in the building wants her advice. In our church communities, it's the seasoned, wise, spiritual lady who leads the Bible study everyone wants to join or the worship leader who's dressed to the nines each Sunday. In our neighborhoods, she's the one with the to-die-for wardrobe, well-groomed kids, and a perfect home. Every other woman on the block is wondering how she does it all. Somehow we've convinced ourselves that we are ill-equipped to invest in others until we have our lives together, whatever "together" means.

We all have our own idea of the "perfect mentor," and often this idea is the very thing that keeps us from feeling qualified to step into the role of mentor ourselves. Harriet wasn't living her life trying to check off all the items on the perfect mentor list; she was just living to love the people around her the best way she knew how—and that is what drew me to her and made her the perfect person for me to learn from.

We Can Just Talk

I loved meeting with Harriet to talk about relationships, dreams, and my hopes for a family. As our friendship grew over time, I realized I wasn't striving to replicate her life; I simply wanted someone to show me what was possible for my own future. And that's the beauty of a mentoring relationship. The expectation of mentorship is not that a mentor will relay everything she knows so you can make a carbon copy of her life. The goal is to show you how she navigates the ins and outs of day-to-day life in the hopes that you can glean from what she's learned and create similar habits—or forge an even better path.

Don't we all want better for those who come after us? I think we do.

As I've built my adult life over the years and worked at creating a home and atmosphere I'm proud of, I look around and see Harriet's fingerprints everywhere. She's present in the way I host the many friends and visitors who come through my door. She's present in the way I cultivate the atmosphere of the day-to-day life under our roof. My heart goes back to all those weekends at her kitchen table every time I see my friends sharing a meal in my dining room. I think back to her every time a friend thanks me for the way I hosted their stay at our house.

Harriet and I went on to meet a few times a month for the next few years. And even though we've both moved to new cities and live a thousand miles apart, we easily pick up right back where we left off when we're together. Our mentoring relationship became a friendship I know we both cherish. Even when we catch up now,

I still feel like I can learn and grow from watching someone a few steps ahead of me. The way she generously gives of her life inspires me to create something beautiful with mine.

Start Where You Are

Harriet modeled the concept of *starting before you're ready*. Because let's be real, when are we ever at a place where we think it's time to start offering our wisdom to the world? While, yes, I sensed Harriet's hesitation, I knew she was exactly what I needed. Hear me: Start before you're ready. Say yes to mentoring even when you think you don't make the cut.

Everyone starts somewhere. I certainly wasn't "qualified" to step into the role of a mentor when I inherited the leadership of a group of more than 30 girls my freshman year of college. I was supposed to guide them through four transformative years of high school, but I still had big questions myself. I certainly didn't have it all figured out. Yet I knew I wanted to show up, whether I felt qualified or not. This was an opportunity to use what I'd already learned from those who had gone before me. And most of that consisted of showing up, serving, and creating a space for people to be themselves.

I realized my "yes" wasn't contingent on whether I was qualified. And I knew I wouldn't be doing this alone. As I mentored, I still had trusted mentors who could come alongside me if ever a roadblock arose. The only thing required of me was to show up with openness and generosity. And that's what I learned from Harriet. I didn't need to *be* anything to step into this mentorship role; I could throw out that checklist I'd been using to disqualify myself from stepping up and simply do it. My life was impacted for the better when Harriet agreed to invest in my life on a regular basis.

When it comes to being a mentor, ditch all the qualifications you think you need. Can't be a mentor until you're making a certain salary? *Wrong.* Can't be a mentor until your home is immaculate? *Wrong.* Can't be a mentor until you have perfect peace in every relationship? *Wrong.* Can't be a mentor until you're an expert in your field? *Wrong.* The only qualification necessary in mentorship might sound cheesy, but it's true: All you need is a willing heart.

Remember, every person in your life is there for a reason. Look around and think about the people you can learn from. Think about those to whom you can pass along your wisdom. No matter how unsure you feel, you might be more effective than you know.

I want mentorship to be accessible and normal to everyone. Mentorship isn't just something we seek out in a career transition or at the beginning of a faith journey; it's something we should seek to have in every season of our lives. And guess what—opportunities are everywhere! If we want to see a generation of women mentoring one another, learning from one another, and collaborating instead of competing, we have to stop waiting and start stepping into this role whether or not we feel qualified.

> If we want to see a generation of women mentoring one another, learning from one another, and collaborating instead of competing, we have to stop waiting and start stepping into this role whether or not we feel qualified.

Like everyone else, I too have wrestled with the idea of whether I should step into the role of a mentor. Some days I feel totally in over my head. For example, a woman who had been a VP at Coca-Cola once joined my business incubator—a space where I mentor business owners in their early phases of development. How could I teach her something she didn't already know? Other times I've encountered women a few years younger than me who taught me so much more in a given conversation than I could ever teach them, often leading me to ask myself, "Shouldn't you be mentoring me?" But time after time, I've learned to trust that women who choose me as a mentor do so for their own good reasons, whatever they might be. And instead of jumping the gun and disqualifying myself, I do my best to step up and see what I can offer in this new friendship and where it might go!

As Harriet and I built a friendship that transitioned from me being one of her kids' friends to a mentor-mentee relationship, we bonded over our shared love of the same people. I learned so much from her through simple conversation. There were no guided lessons; we simply sat across the table from each other and shared life experiences. Similarly, the girls who have asked me to step in as a mentor to them have also become dear friends, often teaching me as much as I taught them and creating a reciprocal relationship where we each learn from the other and grow. What better way to become our best selves than by surrounding ourselves with amazing examples of women who love radically, cultivate incredible relationships, and build purposeful lives. This is the type of connectedness people are yearning for.

Harriet was the queen at facilitating connectedness. She showed me that fostering community and bringing mentorship to the table doesn't have to be overdone. Like the laundry list of qualifications we need to abandon, we also don't need the fanciest china or the biggest house. All we need is to create a space for others to vulnerably enter and lay down the burdens they've been carrying.

The relationships where you can just "be" together have proved in my life to be the most life-giving and richest. Much like I learn from my friendships over an extended period of time, the lessons that often unfold in a mentoring relationship come in the little moments, the nuances of conversation where I pick up one golden nugget or another. By far, simple yet powerful approaches to mentorship have been the most meaningful in my life. I can learn facts and figures at a conference, but life-on-life mentorship turns out to be a much more organic and fulfilling process for me. Harriet showed me how to invite people to the tablescape of my life. My table isn't decorated with Pinterest-worthy floral arrangements—it's just me there, on an average day, and all are welcome. I'll tell you everything I know with no pretense about it. Just come and sit for a while.

> Mentorship is more about what you foster—the trust and the connectedness you build together—than about having all the answers.

The way Harriet invested in my life deeply influenced my own mentoring style. Over the years, I haven't been the step-by-step, check-things-off-the-list kind of mentor. My style is really more the role of a coach. I believe in holding space for the person right in front of me and that it's important for me to let them in on my own journey and cultivate community—much like how Harriet let me peek into the windows of her home and her world. In this way, a mentee and I can both share and learn from each other along the way.

This togetherness and true connectedness flows out of community, and community is where you start allowing someone to speak into your life. Just as Harriet cultivated community around her table and in her home, I have found great joy in opening my home as a welcoming place to others and have seen the fruit that comes when people find a space to truly be themselves and show up together.

Maybe it's time for you to throw perceived "qualifications" out the window. Who gets to decide who can be a mentor and who can't? No one! When I've stepped out into areas where I felt uncertain or unqualified, I've found the greatest break-through. I want the same for you.

Expectations

One thing I loved about meeting with Harriet was her confidence in who she was and what she had to offer. It might have seemed ordinary to the outside world, but her willingness to cultivate a life of love and hospitality was what I wanted to emulate. I didn't seek to learn from her because she looked like she was perfect; I wanted to be her mentee because of the way she made me feel.

My expectations with Harriet were never to fill one specific role, but only to glean from her wisdom. And I said as much when I asked her to be my mentor. I made it clear that I wasn't expecting a ton of time and attention—I just wanted to connect in a very informal way. If we're going to do mentorship well, we need to set expectations, and a key expectation we have to lay down is the notion that a mentor will be perfect. Now, you might have just read that sentence and thought, *Of course! No one is perfect.* But we often come to the table with unspoken or subconscious expectations for who a mentor should be and how they should show up without ever mapping out what that will truly look like.

Let's address some potential expectations people might have for mentors they invite into their lives. Do any of these thoughts sound familiar?

- I want a mentor who has a flawless life.

- I want a mentor who reaches out to me as much as I reach out to her.

- I want a mentor who doesn't judge me.

- I want a mentor who follows through with our plans.

- I want a mentor who is real and honest.

These expectations are reasonable enough (except the first one, of course). But amid a wider array of possible expectations and needs that vary depending on your unique story and experiences, how could a mentor ever know your exact needs without your communicating them? I'm preaching to myself here; I've had my fair share of expectations dashed with both mentoring relationships and friendships. Putting yourself out there in *any* capacity comes with this possibility!

Shortly after we married, my husband and I moved to Colorado to be closer to two dear friends, Katherine and Justin. Katherine and I have been best friends for years and, having grown up together in Tennessee, she and I shared deep roots.

Now this couple had lived in Colorado for years prior to our moving there, and as we transitioned from a long-distance friendship to a much closer involvement in one another's daily lives, linking arms in both life and ministry, we sat down to talk about expectations. I, of course, said I didn't have any. I said I loved others with no strings attached. But oh, how things can change when a subconscious expectation isn't met.

When my best friend missed my birthday party, even though it was because of a previous commitment, I was angry and bitter. It turns out I *did* have expectations! I just didn't know what they were or how to voice them until they were missed. And when I expressed my hurt to her, she was blindsided.

I had convinced myself that I truly had no expectations, but all the while, they existed below the surface, and I hadn't been able to put words to them.

This experience highlighted the importance of getting clear about my needs and the needs of others. I wish that, when I'd had the opportunity, I'd taken the time to consider my expectations more carefully. Now my friends' willingness to ask me about my expectations reminds me to do the same thing as a mentor and a mentee.

A conversation about expectations doesn't have to be awkward or difficult. It's simple: Ask what the person's expectations are of you and of your time together. Then share what your expectations are. That way, you can work toward being on the same page.

If, though, you can't think of any expectations—or like me, you assume you don't have any—think back to times when you've been disappointed by someone in a mentor or mentee relationship or in any kind of relationship. Those disappointments provide a strong clue about your internal hopes and desires—especially the ones you struggle to articulate.

Have you been frustrated when a mentee showed up late consistently? Tell future mentees how much you value starting on time. Have you been hurt when mentors failed to respond to voice mails, emails, or texts? Let your potential mentor know, and if they don't value strong communication as much as you do, choose a new mentor.

While this experience transpired in the context of a friendship, it taught me that people, friends, *and* mentors are not mind readers, and they can't show up for you if they don't know what you need. Even when they do know what you need, they most likely can't nail what you want 100 percent of the time. There's no way on earth they can fulfill every role you have mapped out for them in your mind.

Take Perfection off the Table

It's easy to daydream about the perfect mentor. You see the woman at church who seems to be in charge of everything, and you know she could toss a nugget or two of wisdom your way if you could only get coffee with her every week. Or you notice that woman in your industry who seems to be crushing every metric and goal in sight. What if she just told you everything she knew?

If you *do* get the opportunity to sit down with a woman you've put on a pedestal from afar, I'm sure it will be magical the first time around—or even the first few times around. But if you spend enough time with her, you'll probably come to realize there are areas of her life that aren't as polished as they appear. Sitting across the table from her, you might discover that while she's excelling in her career, her marriage is in the gutter. Or while she manages to show up like Superwoman at church, her family gets the very worst version of her on Sunday afternoons.

No mentor you idealize from afar will be perfect. When you get up close and personal with anyone, mentors included, you'll see the not-so-great parts of their lives. That's because they're *human*. But that's why I'm putting such an emphasis on setting healthy expectations. Even if other parts of their lives are far from perfect, the mentor sitting across the table from you can certainly pour her wisdom from a specific area into you so you can apply it to your life.

Just like a friend or a partner, a mentor can never "complete" or "fix" you, and it would be unhealthy to expect that. Your goal should be to learn about whatever you admired in her in the first place, not to expect her to meet every need in your life. She won't be able to answer every question, and she won't always get it right. The best mentors are also willing to say, "I don't know." And hopefully, they follow that up with, "But I'll figure it out with you!"

A mentor isn't a genie in a bottle to be used at your beck and call. She's a person who's kind enough to share the wisdom she's gleaned from the miles of life she's walked—and she's being generous to allow you to step into her shoes to shortcut your distance. Having realistic expectations with your time, relationship, and capacities can set you up for success.

You don't need to wait around for Brené Brown or Oprah to step into your life. And if they did, would you believe me if I told you they're not perfect either? Leave room for your mentor to be human. And when someone lets you down, don't assume it means something about their identity or their ability to pour into you. It's on *you* to learn from others, and you can learn from anyone. I promise you that.

So I urge you to stop waiting and look around you. Who are you connected to? What do you admire about her? Will you ask her to mentor you in that one specific area? Often the perfect mentor is the woman in your life who's showing up in the day-to-day journey of her family, her friends, her church. She might not be taking center stage, but she's willing and ready to let you come alongside her as she journeys through life.

If perfection is the measure of a good mentor, we'd all be out of luck. And "having it all together" could be the very thing holding you back from stepping into the role of a mentor as well. The idea that you have to be perfect before being qualified to lead is a debilitating lie.

So let's stop disqualifying ourselves and others when looking for a mentor. Let's take *perfection* off the list of qualifications, because I guarantee you will be searching forever if that's the main qualifier.

Extend grace to yourself and extend it to others. Whether you're a mentor or a mentee, the best gift you can give is showing up—imperfections and all.

—— Questions for Discussion and Reflection ——

1. Have you ever had a relational mentor who focused more on connectedness than on discipleship? Was this approach impactful for you?

2. Does anyone around you foster community well? What would it look like to ask her to mentor you in this area?

3. What have you had on your list of qualifications for a mentor? Which of those qualities might you need to abandon?

4. Do you feel qualified to be a mentor? Why or why not?

* * * * *

Action Step: Make the bold move this week: *Ask*. Seek out a woman you admire and invite her out for coffee and conversation. Tell her one aspect of her life that you want to emulate and ask her to share her experience in that area with you.

MENTORS LEAD BY EXAMPLE

SIX

Lucy

Rigorous course loads in college weren't exactly my thing, and although I was attending school on an academic scholarship, the four-year window for pursuing my degree could be summed up in one short but oh-so-important word: *fun.*

The summer before college, I was on the hunt for a part-time job that would accommodate my fall's demanding social calendar and exhaustive global studies degree course load. (Can you hear the sarcasm here?) In reality, I needed work that would allow me to log in only a few hours a day and still have a good time—plus have a bit of space to do my homework, because, let's face it, that global studies degree wasn't going to earn itself.

In my small town, where the town square was and is still a thing and everybody knew everybody's business, finding a gig by word of mouth wasn't a challenge. A friend connected me to a couple for whom she'd babysat the year before. She wanted to pass along the position to someone she trusted.

I knew the family by reputation. They had two daughters my age and a younger son, the one I'd be babysitting. Meeting one another for the first time was pleasant. We quickly hit it off and determined my start date. But what was meant to be just a breezy college-era job became so much more—it was a divine appointment.

If we truly believe every season is a steppingstone for the next, then this season would be one of my biggest preparations toward stepping into my biggest dreams for the years to come. Watching Lucy taught me I didn't have to choose. I could ride the tension of having both a career and a family. And that sure, sacrifices would be involved, and it wouldn't always be perfectly balanced. But no matter what message Christian culture or mainstream media wanted to send my way, I could have both.

Front-Row Seat

This season of my life continually reminded me that holding the dream of a thriving family and flourishing career in tandem was possible. And it provided me with a front-row seat to watch one woman deftly spinning the various life plates I so hoped I would one day learn how to balance, myself. She had it all: a family I admired, friendships that ran deep, and a respectable career. In my eyes, Lucy had nailed this juggling act.

As with a few of my other mentoring relationships, Lucy wasn't a formal mentor; we didn't have outlined discussions. Our relationship was founded on something much more important. She was entrusting me with serving her family, and this allowed me into one of the most sacred places in her life—her home.

Lucy and her family gave me such a gift as I observed their life unfolding in the mundane day-to-day. I helped cart around my main man, JR, and he affectionately called me his "man sitter" because after year one of my "babysitting" him, I'm pretty sure he was taller than me.

For me, the ability to watch the routines of a family I respected was a blessing added to what I thought would be just a job that funded my outings with friends on Friday nights. Lucy and her family may believe I'm painting an over-the-top picture, but their life was what an ideal family living under one roof looked like to me: happy, connected, and with an array of work passions, extra-curricular activities, and community involvement.

Of course, it wasn't rosy all the time. I was there the first time they handled a conversation on sexuality and respect for women, I was there when we had to navigate learning disabilities, and I was there when we had health scares. I was there for the mundane moments, but I was also there for the big moments that counted. I had a front-row seat to witness how every type of circumstance, big and small, could be handled as a family—together.

I dreamed of someday having both a deeply connected family *and* a career, but messages all around me made me wonder if that was possible. Yet in that season, I was given a ringside view for how to do it well, learning from a family I grew to love and admire that cultivated a space of openness and connectedness unlike any I'd ever seen. But that was just the beginning for me. Lucy was excelling in the career department as well. While managing a bustling family schedule, she also had a flourishing career, working as an adviser at the liberal arts college at my university.

Like most of us, she didn't start out at the top. She went back to school to earn her doctorate years back while still having two young daughters. She sacrificed a lot to make family and career work together—but she did it. And through this, she showed me the delicate balance of being present with her kids and working outside the home, and how to work through the sacrifices that accompany this balance.

I saw Lucy manage her time well. She was present to the task at hand, whether she was meal prepping to make evenings less stressful, working on homework with her son, or fielding an after-hours work call. She modeled how healthy boundaries are necessary, sometimes turning down social invitations to prioritize family time, other times allowing her job to take a front seat. She certainly didn't have more time in the day than the rest of us, but she made it work because she made her yeses count.

She's Got It All

People around town loved Lucy. If you met her at a cocktail party, it would be easy to think she had it made. She had a happy and healthy family, a thriving social life, and a husband who was a doctor—what a dream!

And she was living the dream. But I once heard Lucy and her husband, Warren, talking about the season when she worked to put him through medical school. Talk about a tough season. When I later remembered that conversation, I found the encouragement to keep going during the first five years of my marriage, a time when I was working hard to build a business from the ground up and put *my* husband through school at the same time. Often sacrifices must be made to make a career and family work. There are seasons for running and seasons for resting. If you want both, you have to accept it's never going to be perfectly balanced. But you can do it with grace, and that's what Lucy showed me.

While working under Lucy's wing, I also witnessed how a family with two high-achieving and full-time working parents could remain connected, engaged, and successfully manage life. This was such a treasure, because that was a future I wanted. Lucy's life was such a relief to me because it showed me there was a better way. Our world harbors such polarizing views about a woman's place in the world and shames her from every side. Not all women want the same things. How could we? We are all unique and can make our own choices. I knew I needed someone to show me how to walk out the life I wanted, and Lucy pointed the way.

The older I've become, the more I've noticed that my male counterparts don't question whether they can have it all—a family *and* a career. But almost every woman I know does. They may not outwardly discuss whether they can, but we all ask ourselves, *Can I really make it work?* We're often the ones planning to adapt, accommodate, and adjust for our families. I've been doing this since the early days of my business, planning for those years when I'll be a mom.

Even as a millennial, I've had girlfriends look at me over lunch and gasp, "You're not planning to stay home with your kids? You're going to let someone else raise them?" I'll want to be a little more hands off with the business and more hands on with the kids— sure. But my plan is to raise them *while* I also have a career I'm passionate about.

Of course, this is *my* dream. Many women dream of staying home to raise their children. Neither path is wrong. That's what's so beautiful about this life—we get to make these choices for ourselves and our families! But the idea that we should be aghast over women choosing to work—even over those who *need* to work to provide for their kids—has got to go. I'm grateful I had the opportunity to see a career-driven mom living her life on her terms and doing it so well. I'm grateful for Lucy.

Each Moment Is an Opportunity

Every single season can be used as a learning opportunity. We can learn from the good, the bad, and everything in-between. Think of each experience as a steppingstone for what comes next. In my case, babysitting wasn't part of my long-term plan. Because let's be honest, being a babysitter isn't the most glamorous job.

I mean, is it ever easy being a fun babysitter yet still holding your ground as an authoritative figure? Or dealing with tantrums, sibling drama, and the teenage transition years? You love those kids so much, and yet they're not your children. You have a voice, but how much voice do you have before you're stepping over boundaries?

But that's just it—even when you're in a role that might look a little different than your long-term dreams, you can still harness it as an opportunity to learn. Maybe you're wondering why you are where you are in life. Maybe you're thinking you're supposed to be a lot further along in achieving your dreams. I can empathize, because I've felt that too.

But here's what I've learned from the seasons in life that might not be on the highlight reel: We can learn just as much if we look at the bigger picture. Whatever we're doing, we can look for what our circumstances might be doing for us and in us rather than focusing on what they're not. My time in Lucy's home was a catalyst and blueprint for what I did want in ten years—both a thriving family and a successful career. And through my time in Lucy's home, I got to witness a real-life example of the life I wanted and learn how I could lay a solid foundation for my own family while pursuing my career dreams. Each moment is an opportunity to learn, and this was one that shaped me into the businesswoman I am today and the mother I will be in the future.

As I've gone on to be a mentor to other women, I've taken a

note or two from Lucy. I've tried to empower younger women to recognize that they don't have to choose between a career and family. Just like their male counterparts, they can be excellent parents, excellent partners, and run full speed after their passions—never questioning if one has to take a permanent backseat.

In many ways, like Lucy, I've learned to model this more than just say it. She showed me that I can hold multiple dreams in tandem, sometimes making sacrifices but never fully laying them down. And I hope to pass that on to the women coming behind me. So today I'm fiercely pursuing a rockin' marriage, doing the emotional work necessary to lay a foundation for welcoming children into my family, and going full speed in my career. It's important to me that the women coming behind me see me living out my calling, like I saw through Lucy, rather than just hearing me talk about it.

Celebrating One Another

So many loud voices say when you become a wife, you need to lay down everything else to be "godly." Others say you can't be a present mom if you don't stay home with your kids full-time. Or if you travel for work, you're opening the door for disconnection from your husband. And conversely, our modern hustle culture leaves many stay-at-home moms feeling as if their role isn't important or not a "real" job. But ladies, we've got to learn to celebrate one another!

If staying home with your kids to prioritize connection or deciding not to travel to maintain intimacy seems essential for your family, by all means, make those choices! Kudos to you for making that happen—I celebrate you in that choice. And if running after your career with an innate passion to leave your mark on the world lights you up, do that! Both paths are praiseworthy and equally important if that's the lane to which you feel called. One person's way isn't synonymous with *the right way*.

It's time that we women start championing one another in the personal—and *different*—decisions we're making. Let's stop critiquing one another. Find the people who encourage you on your journey, and seek to pour into others as you help them on their way.

Eventually, we're going to wake up and realize that we're pretty worn down from listening to all the voices. When we start relying on guidance from the masses instead of finding a mentor who can adequately model the life we have a conviction to pursue, we can feel pulled in a hundred directions.

Yes, you can have an amazing career *and* a connected marriage. Yes, you can stay at home *and* feel fulfilled without pursuing a career. Yes, you can travel and make the most with your spouse when you're home only four nights a week. Yes, you can choose not to travel because those simple nights at home are more meaningful to your family and more important than the big adventures away. Again, one person's *way* is not synonymous with *the way*.

Going against the norm isn't comfortable. But because of what Lucy did in the '90s—pursuing her doctorate while raising two little girls and maintaining a strong marriage, all while living in the deep South where a *good mom* was synonymous with a *stay-at-home mom*—I believed I could do it all too.

That meant when others' opinions about balancing career and motherhood differed from mine, I was able to shake off any shame directed at me because I knew what I was called to do. This is what staying in your lane means: being able to celebrate your sweet friend in her choice while charging forward in yours—and never making it mean anything about your identities in the process. It's possible to be obedient in our callings and celebrate one another's unique paths simultaneously.

> We can be obedient in our callings and celebrate one another's unique paths.

What I needed in my walk was for someone to tell me my lane was not just okay but merited and purposed just for me, even though it looked different from a lot of my friends' dreams. And because Lucy showed up for me, and showed me how to do this, I'm able to turn around and champion my mentees in the same way.

Show, Don't Tell

A babysitting job seems pretty straightforward, right? But for me, it was so much more than babysitting. That's because different from what my previous mentors did, Lucy showed me what she'd learned instead of just telling me about it.

Finding someone I would later consider a life mentor was unexpected and unique. Even now, Lucy probably has no idea how much those years impacted me. To be able to watch the life of their family unfold and Lucy and her husband to let me into their parenting process—this was a different type of mentoring, and it was deeply significant for me.

We learn so much more from what's modeled than what's said. Think of a parent-child relationship—children want to see a parent model the behavior they are asked to follow. I wasn't going to keep my room clean if my parents weren't going to do the same!

We can all pinpoint a time when someone told us what to do but didn't model it for us. And we can also think of times when actions spoke louder than words.

The same goes for relationships we encounter as adults. Values modeled through actions are far more meaningful than empty advice. I remember a rare situation when JR, Lucy's son, took me through the ringer. I ended up crying because he wasn't listening to me, but at the same time, I was frustrated because I didn't want to tattle on him. That's a delicate discipline balance when nannying. So because I didn't want to make a big deal of it, I brushed it off. But when Lucy got home, she knew something wasn't right.

I assume JR ended up telling on himself, confessing that he might have been a little bit hard on me that day and not-so-great a listener. It was tough, because we had developed a sibling dynamic, but he still needed to listen to me. Less than an hour after I left, I got a text letting me know the situation had been handled, even though I hadn't said anything about it. The next day, Lucy, JR, and I had a conversation. JR issued a sincere apology, explaining that he understood he was to respect me, yet Lucy made sure he felt respected in the process too.

Lucy didn't give me a rundown on her top parenting tips; she simply modeled for me her approach to disciplining JR through those growing-pains years—doing so in a way that called him to be a better person, not evoking shame or dismay at any point. And because of that, he grew up to be an exceptional young man.

Sometimes watching is how we learn from our mentors. It's not always through a formal relationship with scheduled meetings; sometimes it's a closer peek into their lives. Sometimes we get to learn from people who are vulnerable enough to let someone else in, to allow others to be up close and personal.

Letting People In

Lucy showed me the concept of letting people in. While I don't yet have children, I'm always attracted to friends and mentors who allow me to see into their lives without feeling pressure to make it all perfect when I'm around. I love when married couples share stories about the knock-down, drag-out fight they had over something like the placement of the laundry basket that morning. I love when friends share stories about how their kid got in trouble for cussing at school. Perfection doesn't make a great story—real life does.

Take inventory of the people already around you. You may not need to go out looking for a mentor; you might just need to open your eyes a little wider and change your perspective. Become a student of an employer or peer you admire. Begin interacting with others with a heart yearning to listen, observe, and learn. Not only will you have the opportunity to glean and learn from the wisdom of others (and maybe even from their mistakes), but you can become a better mentor to those entrusted to you later down the road.

> Interact with a heart yearning to listen, observe, and learn.

Keep your eyes out for people *you* can influence as well. Lucy taught me so much about how I can show up for the people in my immediate sphere. Who are the people in your circle of influence? With whom are you interacting most closely at home or at work? While you might not be playing the role of a formal mentor for them, they're learning from you. Give those people your best.

—— Questions for Discussion and Reflection ——

1. Who has let their life be a guide for yours even though they weren't an official mentor to you?

2. Can you think of anyone who models the lifestyle you want to live?

3. Think about your current life situation. From whom can you learn right now? For whom can you set an example?

4. In this moment, how are you working toward creating the life you envision for yourself? What is holding you back?

5. What do you believe about "having it all"? What does that phrase mean to you?

• • • • •

Action Step: This week, take some time to write down the names of women *already* in your life whose paths you admire. Then start the conversation—reach out to one of them and share how much you admire the path she's taken and why.

When a Potential Mentor Says No

But she might say no! This is what we all dread. Just the thought of it brings on the anxiety sweats and can prevent us from reaching out to ask someone to mentor us.

When I have conversations about finding a mentor with other women, I hear this objection to moving forward time and time again. And trust me, I'm no stranger to this fear myself. While I have had success in asking mentors to step into my life, I've also had a few letdowns.

Is it awkward when a desired mentor says no? Absolutely. It can even be crushing at first. But you can recover. Also, you have to keep the situation in perspective; don't make the "no" mean something bigger than it is. When it comes to approaching a prospective mentor for the big ask, be willing to accept a no. And when it inevitably comes, in some way or another, try not to take it personally.

> Don't make the "no" mean something bigger than it does.

I get it—those moments are awkward. And they may even cause you to shy away from ever asking someone for guidance again. But I promise it's worth getting back in the saddle and mustering up the courage to ask. The reward when someone *does* say yes far outweighs the risk of someone saying no.

A Member of the Club

To illustrate that no one is immune to rejection, let me tell you a little story about when someone said no to me before I could even ask.

It was my second year of trying to break into the author/speaker world, and I was beginning to realize there were these little cliques of women who hung out together and rallied for one another.

I so badly wanted in! I wanted to be a part of what I lovingly like to call the Cool Girls Moms Club.

I called their alliance this because, in my world, it seemed like the late-thirties, early-forties group of women embodied the epitome of success. They were old enough to be respected for having something wise to say, yet they were young enough to have many years left in their careers. They were at the "sweet spot." Every podcast interview I seemed to hear was filled with their stories and comments like, "I would have had nothing to say at 29! I'm so glad I wrote my book ten years later."

Younger than they were, I felt totally unequipped to step into my calling because of comments like that. But there I was doing it, so I figured their guidance would at least give me the qualifications to move forward. I was certain that being taken under their wing would mean I was going to make it. I dreamed of being invited to the conferences they hosted or to be a guest on the podcasts they produced. I dreamed of them mentoring me, championing me, and helping me navigate the murky waters of the publishing and speaking world.

I ended up at an event where I met a woman I would later grow to admire deeply. I had no idea of the breadth of her influence when I met her. She had a lot of questions about the services I offered at the time, and I figured I could learn a thing or two from her as well. We talked about linking arms, and she eagerly expressed a desire for a reciprocal relationship. She would help me with a facet of my career, and I would help her with some projects and new endeavors she was working on.

It sounded like a win-win! She told me to email her and we'd figure out the details. This was a conversation that happened face-to-face, and our connection seemed promising for our future partnership.

After getting home, I emailed her, and, guess what. Crickets. *Surely, she will get back to me*, I thought. So I waited. And waited. And waited. But no, she ghosted me. Actually, it was worse than that. She ghosted me at first, and then she had her *assistant* reply to me explaining that she was busy.

How embarrassing—I felt like I was annoying her, even though she was the one who suggested I email her. When we met, the two of us dreamed up how we could help each other, and she seemed so eager and willing to come alongside me. I had no idea what had happened between our in-person exchange and this turn of events.

And then my mind started doing that thing it always does in these situations—spiraling. *What changed her mind? What does this mean about me?* We all know those voices that start to creep in: *Was I annoying? Should I not have sent a follow-up email? Did I cross a line? Did she think I just wanted something from her? What if no one wants to invest in me? What if I'm "that girl" in my industry?*

I tortured myself at first; I let these negative thoughts run rampant and told myself a lot of negative stories about why she didn't want to be my mentor. The thoughts consumed me, and I had trouble focusing on anything else. But at some point, I had to stop and say, *No more.*

Instead of continuing to spin on the carousel of negative thoughts, I reflected on the abundance of situations where a mentor *did* say yes to me. Furthermore, I reminded myself that I had to take this woman's words at face value. She had seemed genuinely interested when we were face-to-face. So when my mind started going down those winding roads, I just needed to remember that she *had* originally initiated the partnership. I could just take that for what it was worth. Her lack of response didn't mean anything about me. And it didn't mean that I was unqualified to run in her circles or that everything I had worked for up to that point was invalid.

When it became clear to me that these women were not going to be that tribe for me—maybe one day as peers but certainly not as mentors—it stung. Situations like this take you back to fourth grade when you were picked last for kickball. You start to wonder if you're going to be hidden and unnoticed for the entirety of your career—or your life, for that matter. The thought, *Why don't they ever pick me?* is bound to float through your mind in these instances.

But in these moments, remember that it's okay if they don't pick you. It doesn't say anything about you, and it probably doesn't mean much about them either. If you zoom out and allow yourself to see the bigger picture, you'll see it's probably less about them not noticing how awesome you are and more about the fact that they're stretched super thin and don't have the capacity to say yes.

Maybe this woman didn't have the bandwidth. Maybe she got excited when she was dreaming up things face-to-face, only to realize she couldn't follow through because of prior commitments or a lack of time. Maybe she was going through a season where she was having to say *no* a lot more than usual so she could say *yes* to what was most important.

It's so easy to make negative assumptions when our plans don't work out the way we think they should. But all those fears and negative thoughts consuming me? They weren't true. I wasn't annoying, and I didn't simply want something from her. I was offering to serve her in a mutually beneficial relationship. And because other women had chosen to invest in me, I knew I wasn't a person in my industry no one liked. I knew all these things!

Of course, it was crushing to be accepted and then have that acceptance seemingly revoked. I finally thought the Cool Girls Moms Club was going to reach down and offer a

> Guidance—not validation—is the key to our success, and that isn't dependent on one person.

hand up. But poof, that hand was gone. Yet I learned an important lesson through that process. I didn't get the validation I yearned for at that point, but I still went on to succeed.

I *love* having the guidance of a mentor, and validation from others is always a bonus. But that validation in no way moves the needle when it comes to our destiny. Guidance—not validation—is the key to our success, and that isn't dependent on one person.

Build a Bigger Table

Asking is how you find your people. It might take hearing *no* a few more times—some more anxious sweating and awkward situations—but they *are* out there. Whether in the context of friends or mentors, not every relationship will work out. But you have to put yourself out there to find out who *is* a good fit for you. Expect a lot of trial and error with some rejection sprinkled in along the way.

And keep those rejections in mind as you go on to mentor others. Though this experience stung, it illustrated how I want to show up differently for the girls coming a few steps behind me. Shirley Chisholm is known for saying, "If they don't give you a seat at the table, bring a folding chair." I would expand that to say that if you create your own community, you can build a table big enough for everyone hoping for a place to belong. You can invite people already in your life to join you around it. And when people say no to your invitation, keep inviting—your tribe will come. Jesus Himself experienced this! He was rejected by the Pharisees, but He built His own table for the apostles and sinners and those whom society had rejected.

In my experience, choosing to forge ahead despite setbacks always works out for the best. In another case, a mentor dropped me after a few calls because our relationship no longer benefited her. But then someone a lot more intentional stepped in. She was a better fit, and she truly showed me how I want to show up in my career space over the next few years.

> If you create your own community, you can build a table big enough for everyone hoping for a place to belong.

The reality is that people will say no to you—or worse, not follow through after they say yes. But those rejections, painful as they may be, make room for the *right* people to step into your life. So don't make those moments that didn't work out mean something personal. At some point, you, too, will be unable to step into someone's life for one reason or another. We all have to say no sometimes.

My hope for all of us who seek mentors is that, when we're told *no*, we won't read some deeper meaning into it. We won't take it as some scary indicator of our worth or value but simply accept it. It's just a *no*. And a *no* can propel us toward what is meant for us next, something better than what we could ever plan for ourselves.

> Rejections, painful as they may be, make room for the *right* people to step into your life.

MENTORS BREAK
THE MOLD

SEVEN

Karen

My college years flew by with Lucy, Kay, and Harriet helping me to grow into the adult woman I aspired to be. Those three women were role models for how I wanted to live as a wife, mom, and career woman. But none of us were prepared for what was ahead of me—navigating the intersection of faith and marriage. Yikes.

The merging of two lives is never simple. Though you've anticipated newlywed bliss, you start discovering points of contention where neither party is willing to budge. Finding those points so soon after the ceremony is, to say the least, *unexpected*.

I'd say "unexpected" just about sums up what the first year and a half of marriage felt like for us. While I idealistically envisioned easy years filled with starry eyes, a perfectly decorated home, dream jobs, and friendships that felt deeply connected—I was in for a rude awakening. In the midst of trying to figure out how to juggle a not-so-dreamy budget and an uncertain career path, our biggest pain point as a couple soon became apparent—church.

This is not to say that we didn't figure out how to resolve certain issues. We navigated quite a few hard situations in those early years, such as a death in the family, mental health battles, and exposed secrets. But when it came to church, we were supposed to be united. This was supposed to be what came easy. After all, we both loved God.

So why did church have to be so polarizing? We absolutely could not find a middle ground and settle on a church we both loved.

I thought David and I had to be the only couple in the world—and in ministry, no less!—having knock-down, drag-out, screaming fights about our thoughts on church and how it was done. This had to be something only he and I couldn't figure out, an isolated incident among my friends. They all seemed to agree that their churches were a perfect fit, with the sweetest small group and the best Sunday worship routines, followed by Instagram-able brunches. And then there was us—two people *in ministry together* who couldn't seem to get on the same page about church.

On the outside we looked like the model citizens of church attendance. We'd volunteer 30-plus hours a week—as is common for young, eager people looking to be in ministry. But on the inside, we were on the road to spiritual burnout. I sensed the shift, but it would take a few years for my husband to process this. The whole situation seemed like a disaster in the making, and of course, I did myself no favors with my levels of catastrophizing. I was certain this was going to be our demise. If we weren't perfectly on the same page about this, was our marriage doomed?

The worst part was that we never imagined faith would be our biggest point of contention when dating. Like so many young couples, David and I fell head over heels for each other, and we were certain we were *exactly the same*. I mean, we just had *so much in common*. At least that was the idealistic bliss in which we lived for a while. But that myth was busted.

Before we tied the knot, David and I happily went to two separate churches in town, but we intended to find a church home together once we got married. The first roadblock, then, came as we decided which church that would be.

I'll be honest—I was well aware that David's church wasn't a place I could see myself long-term, and I thought our union was going to be my "out." I had even mapped out our next move in my head. (Doesn't that *always* work, ladies?) The beginning of our marriage seemed like the perfect time to transition to a church that was more "us." Together, we could find a community we both loved.

Sure, my husband had been heavily involved in his church—he was even enrolled in their ministry school. But I thought when we got married, we'd find something a little different. And by "different," I mean more *my* style...which I presumed would certainly become *his* style soon enough. My style of church was more mainstream nondenominational, heavy on dissecting Scripture and giving practical lessons to live out. David, meanwhile, loved the freedom of a deeply charismatic church, and he leaned more toward testimonies, stories, and miracles. He was passionate about seeing tangible evidence of the acts of God.

But lo and behold, as we started discerning where we needed to attend as a couple, I had a gut inclination that I should support David and attend his tiny charismatic church. I had peace about the decision, trusting that a sacrifice in this area would lead to a reward I might not be able to see at the moment. But while I'd like to say my heart to honor God encouraged me to have a cheerful attitude, I'd be lying if I did. I'd been *certain* God was going to give us the thumbs-up to try another church, but here we were, making the most of where we needed to be.

Making the most of it might be a stretch. I was actually pretty awful.

Don't get me wrong. The people with whom we attended church were incredible. But this trendy, nondenominational gal had found herself in an old-school charismatic, lion-banners-on-the-wall setting. You could expect services to be filled with horns blowing (only charismatic people will truly understand what that means) and three-hour services multiple nights a week. In the span of a year, I had moved from being the golden girl at the coolest church in town to "David's wife" at our new—and to me, weird—church home.

Burnout

To make this worse, like many young couples committed to ministry, we began life at our new church home on a beeline trajectory toward…burnout. We didn't realize it at the time, but we started doing all the things that eventually lead most young people in ministry to quit by the time they hit 30.

Consider this a word to the wise: If you're pouring out endless hours of service without receiving any investment or support in return, you're on the road to burnout. Church leaders are accountable for the health of the church body and staff, and they need to be aware if you're pouring out more than you have to give.

What were we doing? you might ask. Like I said, *all the things*. And we were doing them with no one checking on our emotional, physical, or spiritual health. Anyone who's ever been on staff at a small church knows what I'm talking about.

"Hey, guys, can you be here every Tuesday and Sunday for services?"

Sure!

"We have a conference coming up next weekend. Can you be an usher?"

Of course!

"Every night?"

No biggie!

"Since you guys are so fun, we think you'd make great volunteers for the youth group! You in?"

Totally!

"What about being the evangelism pastor for Friday night outreach?"

Wow, a title? Of course!

You get the idea. While the above examples may seem a bit exaggerated, this was our reality during the first year of marriage. We were struggling to make ends meet with our day jobs, putting my husband through college on a shoestring budget, and volunteering our time 30-plus hours a week. We expected that our commitment would pave the way toward careers in ministry, with investment and guidance from seasoned leaders, but we were wrong.

Reflecting now, what we initially thought was selfless service on behalf of the church was, in fact, quite unhealthy. We didn't know the importance of setting boundaries, and the church leadership took advantage of our 20-something energy levels. The situation made for an unhealthy relationship between us and this church from the start.

An epidemic of people under 30 are leaving the church. I believe that's in large part due to church leaders taking advantage of young Christians who have eager hearts for ministry—young people who will give all they have because they trust their efforts will turn into a career and that the leadership has their best interest at heart. David and I found ourselves in this exact position, and while no one was forcing us to say yes to every invitation, we knew that this was the route we were expected to take if we wanted a full-time ministry career. And this pitfall wasn't unique to our specific church; so many of my close peers were finding themselves wrung dry by the ministry overload all across the country.

Before we realized we were on the path to burnout, David was on a trajectory toward being a traveling minister. He was the golden boy of the church—they actually gave him the title "son of the house." And since I wanted to foster his dreams and help propel him toward those ambitions, we dove *all in,* saying yes to every volunteer opportunity asked of us—even if I was not so cheery in the process.

Do you sense a disaster in the making?

It took hindsight and a move across the country to realize the toll this took on us. But at the time, we just kept our heads down and tried to contribute as best we could—the way we thought everyone expected us to. David had already proven that he would champion me in anything I set my mind to, and I was eager—determined—to be a supportive wife. Now it was his turn, and we were going to invest in his dreams, like he had mine.

But while David was happily chugging along, still saying yes to everything, I was starting to unravel. I wasn't just dissatisfied; I was becoming *bitter.* Church ministry was supposed to be a feel-good job, right? Instead, I felt exploited. Even in light of all we were doing, zero personal connection or discipleship was happening. I had been involved in a relational ministry for years, so I'd seen it done well. But now I had no one willing to invest in me. I couldn't figure out why we were supposed to be there, or what this disconnect meant for my marriage.

Those first few months were brutal, but God soon made it clear why He asked me to trust Him in staying at this church. Another misfit came along…Karen. And I'm so thankful I leaned in and trusted Him because if I had left, I wouldn't be writing this chapter about the impact this dear friend and mentor had on my life.

A Firm Foundation

I began to realize that if there was any way for me to survive ministry, I needed someone to show me how to carve out a path of my own—a *healthy* path for serving with longevity. And I needed someone who might have walked a similar road. Someone who could encourage me in my faith and hold me and David accountable to setting healthy boundaries in ministry. I didn't want to find myself burned out and disillusioned like so many others.

Right at the time when I needed her, Karen showed up as what I can only describe as a lifeline.

If the only reason my gut told me to stay was because I was meant to meet Karen, it was all worth it. She not only showed me how to navigate that season but also became a guide and a true pillar of my faith as I've continued to navigate the murky waters of Christian ministry—a place about which I often find myself wondering, *Do I belong here?*

I first met Karen at a young adult function hosted at her house. This meeting turned out to be a godsend. I had been craving community from my church crowd, and finally, someone was cultivating it! While I know we all can be creators of community, I was stretched pretty thin with volunteer commitments four or five nights a week, and I couldn't take on another responsibility. So I desperately wanted someone from the older, wiser crowd to take an interest in mentoring and discipling the younger crowd…and finally, someone was.

At the first meeting, I was immediately attracted to Karen's blunt, no-nonsense personality. We soon began regularly meeting one-on-one for coffee, and all my honest questions and feelings started pouring out of me. I could no longer hold it all in. I shared the pain of David and me being on separate pages, the exhaustion that was setting in, and how I was hanging on by a thread to my idea of ministry.

Karen provided me with safety and freedom to share my concerns and gave me permission to start setting boundaries—all without judging me as someone who was going off the deep end in her faith.

And that was the beginning of one of my rawest, most honest relationships in ministry to date. I hadn't shared those concerns with anyone but David up to that point. She invested in this tired girl who had bitterness in her heart, listening and empowering me in my honesty rather than hushing my voice and telling me to be the quiet, submissive wife. This became the foundation on which I would form future relationships in the ministry space—a foundation of honesty, openness, and no pretense.

When Two Don't Feel like One

Meeting with Karen gave me the space to really wrestle with my role as a wife. Being in my mid-twenties when we first got married, I was in the throes of trying to figure out who I was while my husband was trying to do the same. I was worried about how I could pursue my own dreams if everything seemed to be about supporting him as he explored ministry as a career. As I looked around, that was all I saw in this setting—wives who tended the kids or traveled with their husbands as they bopped around from church to church. But how would that ever work for my dreams? I had always been career-driven, a huge dreamer, and not the most likely candidate to sit on the sidelines as a cheerleader.

Of course, I wanted my husband to pursue his dreams, just not at the expense of mine or at the expense of being together. But I didn't fit the mold of the wife I needed to be to function in the church we were in.

The reality is, if in that hard season I had dug in my heels and given my sweet husband an ultimatum, he probably would have appeased me. David very much wanted to support and empathize with me, but he was also in a very different space. This was his church home, and it was a community close to his heart. Consequently, it was harder for me to feel he truly understood where I was, and therefore it was harder for me to receive his input on the matter. As hard as this season was, it taught me an important lesson: There will be seasons when not even your spouse can meet you in your pain. You're going to miss the boat with each other, and sometimes you'll need someone else to step in.

Karen was that person for me. She was a sounding board and a voice of wisdom, helping me understand that disagreement didn't mean the collapse of my marriage. She encouraged me to speak honestly to David but also to listen fairly, letting his heart do what it needed to do and giving him space to pursue his dreams in the same way he was giving me space to pursue mine. She helped me trust that my husband and I would end up in sync.

> In some seasons, not even your spouse can meet you in your pain. You're going to miss the boat with each other, and sometimes you'll need wise counsel to step in and point you back to the truth.

Because Karen believed in David and me as a couple, I had hope to see the possibilities rather than the potential downfalls in our marriage. She helped me find ways to use this season for David and me to grow together rather than grow apart. She inspired conversations between us that helped us see each other's perspectives and also learn from each other. These conversations then built trust and honor between us, and over time we became stronger in our marriage—a team not always on the same page but ultimately chasing after the same goal.

Stick with It

The truth is, life is hard. It's so much easier to just run from the discomfort and pain of challenging situations rather than enduring and sticking them out. Under Karen's encouragement, though, I didn't run; I didn't give up. And I'm so glad I didn't! David and I are better together, and in that season, I learned that weathering storms and honoring your commitments—sticking around somewhere you absolutely do not want to be—has benefits that far outweigh the sacrifice.

This time taught me so much about perseverance and breakthrough. Without Karen, I would not have been able to stay standing on my own two feet in that environment. It would have been so much easier to have thrown a fit, left those sequin lion tapestries that covered the church, run for the hills…and asked my husband to sacrifice his dreams in the process. But that would have been pretty selfish, and I wouldn't have received Karen's advice, mentorship, and friendship out of the deal.

God is always good to use the challenging circumstances of our lives, and I realize now how much growth I would have missed out on if I hadn't chosen to stay.

Making a New Mold

Those early years at a church where I felt so out of place made me feel invisible. The staff was characterized by dominant men and sweet, quiet women—except for me and Karen.

Karen and I did *not* fit the mold. We were outspoken, opinionated, and sometimes a bit too aggressive when sharing our opinions. Karen was there to show me how to tone down aggression, to appropriate assertiveness, and to sprinkle in a bit of tact.

And if we're getting real and raw here, this was a valuable lesson for me to learn in my mid-twenties, on the front end of my life. Here I was, wrestling with my identity. Who was I going to be? Was I going to be who everyone wanted or expected me to be within this specific church culture? Or was I going to show up as I truly was—an outspoken, sometimes haphazard gal? Was I going to speak out when I saw practices or ideology that seemed unhealthy and destructive, or would I keep quiet and avoid rocking the boat like my husband might have wished I would do? Was this what the church—a place where everyone is supposedly welcomed—really supposed to be?

Karen showed me how to be fearless in using my voice, and that sometimes it's necessary to rock the boat even when people are telling you to be quiet. Not fitting a specific mold does not make you wrong. As I spoke out, the criticism I received—that my opinions were too much, that I should just sit in the back and keep my mouth shut in the name of tradition—became a refining fire for me. They helped me see my God and my true calling—one empowering women to use their voices—more clearly.

If You See Something, Say Something

While everyone else nudged me to shush, conform, or not rock the boat, Karen was there offering a hand up, saying, "Girl, I've *been* there." And what a breath of fresh air that was when I had previously felt so alone. She not only sympathized with me but empathized because she'd lived through the same experience.

For a while, I felt that Karen and I were just an island to ourselves, watching members come and go in droves as they burned out. I can't describe the immense relief I felt when even more people finally began coming forward—others who were uncomfortable with the unhealthily structured systems created within the church. The health of the church body had been sacrificed to appease a few of the leaders, and as others began to share their experiences, I realized I wasn't the only one feeling both taken advantage of and isolated. Now I began to find the support and community I'd been looking for—people like me who desired to do ministry for the long haul in a healthy and honoring way.

Just because everyone else had *seemed* to be enjoying the process didn't mean I was wrong, yet for so long I felt like I was crazy for thinking the church was asking too much of us. I questioned myself for thinking differently from the group. But when something is off, someone has to be the first to notice. Someone has to be the one to say, "This isn't right." It's okay to notice even minor things that are off, because all those minor issues can contribute to a toxic culture. An absence of moral failures or scandals is not the only indicator of a healthy ministry.

That was one of my first experiences being the odd one out as a result of my opinions and boldness. But it wasn't my last, and forging a new path isn't for the faint of heart. Anyone forging a new way can tell you that doing things differently never comes easy. Pioneers and mold-breakers are often the first to notice when something is meant to be done differently and then wrestle their way through. Church culture is challenging, and having a group of humans leading anything means it's bound to get messy. Asking questions about things that seem off does not make you "crazy." It might make people mad, but seeking the health of the church body in any capacity is vital for the church to grow.

In the end, David and I left that church, understanding that we had different goals from the leadership and it was our time to move on. But I'm glad I stuck it out, because I left stronger and better acquainted with the voice I'd always had. I also left with an extra dose of courage to use when I saw things that didn't sit right with me and a better understanding of what I believed the church should be.

Sometimes your voice will invite dialogue and create change. Other times, however, to continue growing with your convictions, you may have to start peacefully heading in the direction your heart is leading you, even if it means leaving others behind and stuck in old patterns. Not everyone will agree with you, but that doesn't mean you're wrong. It just means you're making a less painful way for others to follow in their own time.

Equipped to Encourage

In those areas where you feel like you've endured a hard facet of life, I challenge you to offer a hand up to someone else who's walking through it. Step in and guide her along the path you took to thrive, not just survive.

Karen helped me keep standing during a hard season. Her hand up helped me not to lose myself in others' quests to keep the peace and conform. She gave me grace to refine, polish, and improve those areas that might still be a little rough around the edges yet stay true to myself and my voice along the way.

Karen's presence in my life saved my faith in the church and showed me a better way of how ministry can and should be done. I was considering walking away from ministry altogether until she stepped in. She modeled for me that I could empower other women to use their voices, even when they feel alone or silenced. Now one of my greatest joys is to step in and help others see they don't have to show up as anyone other than themselves.

Being led by Karen equipped me to step up to the plate in my own mentoring journey and encourage the women I pour into to think twice before they throw in the towel. I remind them that it's okay to speak up when they inevitably find themselves in a place where they hold the not-so-popular opinion—at work, at church, or in their friend groups. It's painful to step into this discomfort. Challenging, yes, but certainly okay. Just because not everyone likes you doesn't necessarily mean you're wrong.

We were each created to have a voice, and never were we meant to silence ourselves to blend in. In some church cultures, this can be really hard to walk out. When you're tempted to blend in, keep in mind what the apostle Paul taught us about the functioning of the church:

> The human body has many parts, but the many parts make up one whole body. So it is with the body of Christ...we have all been baptized into one body by one Spirit, and we all share the same Spirit. Yes, the body has many different parts, not just one part. If the foot says, "I am not a part of the body because I am not a hand," that does not make it any less a part of the body. And if the ear says, "I am not part of the body because I am not an eye," would that make it any less a part of the body? If the whole body were an eye, how would you hear? Or if your whole body were an ear, how would you smell anything?

> But our bodies have many parts, and God has put each part just where he wants it. How strange a body would be if it had only one part! Yes, there are many parts, but only one body. The eye can never say to the hand, "I don't need you." The head can't say to the feet, "I don't need you." In fact, some parts of the body that seem weakest and least important are actually the most necessary (1 Corinthians 12:12-22).

We're all part of one body. If you were created to be a hand, don't let someone else tell you what you need to do to be a foot!

As I mentor, I hope to champion women and help them reap the reward on the other side of grueling perseverance. That doesn't mean encouraging them along toward the happiest, best decisions of their lives at all times. Much of the time, it means remaining a constant companion as my mentees push through the hardest moments of life—setting boundaries with loved ones, choosing to face past trauma head-on, or not letting the inner (or outer!) critic silence their dreams.

But how could I champion other women in their own experiences if I hadn't stuck it out on my own journey and allowed Karen to step in? She showed me how to use my voice when I felt silenced. She demonstrated how I can show up as 100 percent me even when I'm a square peg trying to fit into a round hole, encouraging me to choose to stick with the hard thing when I so desperately want to escape.

I was made to have a voice. I was made to stand tall. But it took Karen coming along to show me that. Without another leader validating that it was okay to be an outspoken woman

> Your voice sets you apart. You were made to belong and simultaneously stand out.

within the church, I may not have had the confidence I needed to rock the boat in other situations where more was at stake. Karen's confidence and boldness were the very things that gave me the strength to look for opportunities to teach others that they, too, have a voice.

—— Questions for Discussion and Reflection ——

1. Have you ever felt like something wasn't right but didn't know how to approach it? How would you handle that same situation today?

2. Has anyone ever rescued you from almost giving up? What are some key characteristics of that person?

3. Think about your current sphere of influence. Do you know someone who needs a defender? Someone who needs you to help her find her voice?

4. Do you have someone in your life with whom you can share honestly without feeling judged? If so, do you meet with her often enough?

· · · · ·

Action Step: This week, think about a woman in your sphere of influence you know is walking through the messy middle or trying to climb out of the trenches. Give her a call or take her out for coffee or dinner, then remind her of her voice and help her face this thing head-on—whatever it might be.

MENTORS FIGHT FOR
YOUR FUTURE

EIGHT

Catherine

don't travel too much.

Or at least that's what I told myself.

Making a pan of brownies every other day isn't a problem. Not for me. I have a fast metabolism, so it's fine, right?

Or at least that's what I told myself.

This was my norm. Finding seemingly okay methods of escape from anything that felt remotely painful or hard. *If life gets tough, just add joy!*

For you, maybe it's watching eight hours of Netflix instead of getting that work done. Or crushing that daily Coke from McDonald's even though the doctor told you your blood sugar is in the high range. I sympathize. I'm all about a fun experience to get through a mundane day or to alleviate the pain of a bad one.

But masking pain is not the same as dealing with it, and moving to Colorado showed me in a whole new way just how much I was coping rather than working through the pain points of my life. At first, it seemed like just another fun life adventure, but I fell back into old patterns—filling my life with *all the things* so I could avoid what I most needed to face. The pain I'd first started dealing with in my conversations with Karen and Kay was still there. That kind of pain is like a chronic illness: You can learn to recognize the signs of a flare-up and gain the tools to manage the symptoms, but it's never really cured.

And in this new season of life, I needed new tools to manage the flare-ups.

A New Season

On a chilly December day, David and I packed everything we owned and said good-bye to the only town I had ever called home. We were eager to build our new life in Colorado, and everyone told us this would be a special season of bonding—the whole "leaving and cleaving" thing. They were right, but what they didn't prepare me for was everything this move would unearth in my heart.

The thrill of a new adventure carried me through our first months there. However, it wasn't long before "the girl who got away" became "the girl who desperately wanted to go back." Although I had experienced exhaustion in Tennessee, I was still *accustomed* to filling every second of every day. But once we settled in Colorado, I realized this was the first season in my life when I was forced to slow down.

In case you think I'm exaggerating, the week before I left Tennessee, I had coffee dates set in two-hour time slots from 7:00 a.m. to midnight. Sure, I had a lot of people to see because I was leaving town, but this kind of schedule was normal for me.

So now, after years of living in the fast lane—stacking a standard week with coffee dates, after-work activities, family commitments, and church events—I found myself in a new town with my first significant "slow season," and I couldn't see an end in sight. This new normal terrified me. And I found it excruciating.

So what did I do? I built a business. If I couldn't pack my days to the brim with family and friend time, I would throw myself into a project. This meant working long hours at my day job and then focusing all my attention on my budding career dreams in the evening.

As I said before, I fell into my old patterns. My impulse was to live life at full speed with no room for assessing where I was physically, emotionally, or spiritually. I knew building a business would challenge me—stretch me, even. But I truly believed that I could power through at my usual pace. I thought I could keep moving without giving my troubled and homesick heart a second glance.

Later I realized I was avoiding something I knew would come to the surface if I stood still: my pain.

Numb

No small contributor to my stress was the fact that I was still a "yes girl." And honestly, that's kind of who I am at my core. I tend to say yes to all the things—yes to that vacation, yes to that business trip, yes to having those people over for dinner, yes to any opportunity to help a friend, even if I'm stretching myself so thin that I'm angry about how busy I am.

Unfortunately, I once again didn't leave myself any margin. We hadn't been in Colorado long before I'd jam-packed my life to the brim with commitments and activities, this time all with ones I truly loved. But without any margin in my life, those activities were no longer enjoyable. And worst of all, when I started to recognize these issues, I chose not to face them head-on. This pattern of behavior cultivated over a lifetime was embedded deep within me. I just kept my head down like the good soldier I was and kept saying yes—yes to all the things.

I slowly became emotionally numb. This numbness wasn't just blocking the negative feelings I was so scared of experiencing, though. It was also preventing me from feeling the happiness this new season was bringing.

About nine months into our life in Colorado, I started to feel burnout again—extreme burnout. I couldn't see what my lightning speed and manic tendencies were doing to my body, and I was no longer capable of feeling overly sad *or* overly happy. My body was telling me something was wrong, yet I didn't want to feel that either.

So what did I do? I picked up the pace! Surely another trip home to reconnect or a long weekend at the beach was the recipe for rejuvenation. And as usual, I could justify why I was living at lightning speed within my business. *Just another business conference—it's education! I have to land this client—I should meet her in person!* And this wasn't untrue. I was spending my time in worthwhile ways, but not in the ways I needed most. What I needed most was to slow down. But slowing down would require facing my feelings. Feelings like pain, fear, sadness. Feelings that every part of me wanted to avoid.

And I think deep inside, I knew that. The problems weren't obvious to anyone else at first, but the stress of putting my husband through school and being halfway across the country from my family, then building my business on top of all that and "doing all the things," was starting to take its toll.

And deep inside was a lot of anger.

The Eruption

One fateful Saturday afternoon, on my way to church, a little incident made me realize how much anger I'd been stuffing down and told me it was time to make some adjustments.

It was such a small thing—someone cut me off in traffic. But anger welled up from deep within me, and this polite, small-town, Southern Christian girl felt the need to roll down her window and let loose a double barrel of fury.

You know the type of road rage you see and think to yourself, *That person needs to get off this road—NOW—and cool down?* Well, I was that person. As soon as I heard the words come out of my mouth, disbelief and shock at my own reaction hit me. At the same time, I felt relief; it was as if I had just let out a mountain of unaddressed anger that had been making its home in me for years. Here was that anger in all its glory. Poor driver. He may not have even realized he'd cut me off, but I sure let him know! Not my shining moment, but wow, did it feel good to just *yell!*

But wait. *Why did that feel good?* This was my first indicator that this happy-go-lucky, free-spirited girl was *angry.* Not just a little angry—a lot angry. All that stuffing down, all that trudging on, had finally erupted.

And I was *tired.* So tired. I'd been burning the candle so quickly at both ends that traffic was making me feel unhinged. The irony didn't slip past me in that moment: Here I was, flipping out, all while on my way to volunteer at church. I had to laugh thinking of my fellow volunteers seeing me in this moment. And at the same time I knew something needed to change.

My knee-jerk reaction of fury was the first thing that clearly told me it was time to slow way down. Of course I should have seen it before this moment, but I was so busy saying yes to things that I was missing the madness making its home inside me. I had spent years losing bits of myself to all the yeses, and it was finally time to say no. No to living life in the fast lane, no to stuffing my life full of just one more good thing, no to the numbness, bitterness, and resentment that was weighing my soul down.

I didn't want to be a woman marked by anger, and I knew if I didn't learn to address my lack of personal boundaries—if I didn't learn to say no to even a few things—this anger and unhealthiness would bleed into every part of my life. And I came to the weightier realization that if I didn't steward my soul, I couldn't carry my dreams nearly as far as I hoped.

So shortly after this outburst, after years of running at this chaotic pace, I decided this would be my season to hit pause. No more traveling, running away, or distracting myself. I needed to commit to living in the present and staying planted, not jumping ship for what might feel better in the moment.

As trivial as it sounds, this decision was brutal. The word that often popped into my head when I felt the deep need to escape all the feelings creeping up was *restraint*. And that's exactly how I characterize that year as I look back—the year of self-discipline *and* restraint. Instead of running to the next thing, I was pressing pause, saying no, and having to trust that the slowness I was incorporating into my life would eventually lead to growth.

> To force yourself to slow down so you can simply *be*—that's a lesson for the books!

That year of slowing down was the kindest gift I could have given myself, but it wasn't exactly comfortable. Any of you compulsive doers who have ever intentionally hit pause know what I mean. To force yourself to pause so you can simply *be*— that's a lesson for the books! But I knew the act of slowing down and committing to feeling everything I had left unfelt would be the key to living a life of true fullness and freedom. It would be a fight, but it would be worth it. And I knew I needed someone to walk this out with me.

Enter Catherine.

A Guiding Voice

Catherine was a therapist who was deeply connected to others within my church circle. I heard testimony after testimony about the freedom my friends had experienced after working with her, so I thought I'd give a session with her a shot.

Catherine has spent her career as a church counselor. She's what I call the Olivia Pope of our church community. All my *Scandal* fans know what I mean—she's everyone's *fixer*. I knew something was wrong, and Catherine was ready to sign up for the hard work. *Fix me*, I said. *I'm tired.*

One session with Catherine turned into two, and two sessions turned into biweekly visits. These sessions didn't start with immediate connectedness or even monumental results, but by taking the small steps of showing up each week, I began seeing the fruit of digging deep, discovering limiting beliefs and lies I had believed, and then replacing them with truth.

Our biweekly appointments changed to weekly sessions for the better part of a year, and Catherine slowly shifted from the simple role of a therapist to a permanent guiding voice in my life. We even traded our talents: She walked me through my limiting beliefs and pain points, and I helped her with the media side of her business. I know that's not typical for a therapist, but her style of practice allowed for this unique relationship, and thankfully, she felt the connection too.

Because of her commitment to helping me "upgrade my

emotional intelligence," I came to understand that only by operating from a place of freedom would I be able to carry my dreams—dreams of being a present and emotionally healthy mother and wife while simultaneously building a diverse portfolio of business and creative projects. Catherine helped me work through my deeply ingrained patterns and coping mechanisms that kept me busy and diverted my focus from the most important things. If I wanted it all—to be a connected mother and wife while also succeeding in my career—I would have to set some boundaries. My current boundaryless life was not setting me up to carry my dreams with longevity.

When I sat down with her early on, I knew our sessions would be uncomfortable—and they were. But after two years of sitting in that chair and delving into the early beliefs I had developed, I was able to build a mental foundation that was sturdy, a house that wouldn't be swayed by storms or shift on the sands of a shiny but numb life.

Looking back at the events that led me to Colorado, it's now quite clear to me that God used whatever means He could to allow me to cross paths with Catherine. My husband and I may have thought we were moving across the country in part to do ministry, but what if this move was for us to be ministered to?

One of my favorite passages from Scripture speaks of God's guidance: "Your word is a lamp to guide my feet and a light for my path" (Psalm 119:105). God doesn't always show us the path 50 yards ahead, but He will most certainly show us the next right step to take. And I'm certain He led me right to meeting Catherine, step by step. She was essential in helping me walk toward my destiny and carry my ever-evolving dreams while operating in as much wholeness and freedom as possible.

This commitment to operating in wholeness meant getting gut-level honest with myself. I had to admit my failures and struggles; I had to surrender my pride. And in asking for my honesty, Catherine empowered me to be a truth teller in all areas of my life. I became more comfortable with the uncomfortable feelings in my soul, feelings I'd spent so many years fighting. Releasing my pride and embracing vulnerability changed me from the inside out, and in the process, I found I not only had more space for all of my own feelings, but I could carry space for others' discomfort and struggle as well.

> God doesn't always show us the path 50 yards ahead, but He will most certainly show us the next right step to take.

God's Timing

They say timing is everything, and I've never doubted that someone can come into my life in just the right season for specific lessons. Lynell showed me what love looks like even when it's costly. Lucy showed me how to balance family and a career so that I could have both. Karen showed me how to thrive in hard seasons. Each woman taught me a pivotal lesson I could carry with me through life.

But Catherine's role was a little different. In most mentoring relationships, the mentor is focused on modeling her own life. Catherine was more focused on helping me see what God was doing in my own life rather than putting her journey on display for me. Her role was more about helping me understand who I was created to be, to pull out the gold that already existed inside of me. She helped me understand my identity in Christ, not offering advice from a place of expertise but serving as a mirror, reflecting the truth of my identity back to me.

Showing Up

As edifying as it was to work with Catherine, at times I felt like I was being broken down to be built back up again. The way she reached in to pull truth out of me was equally rewarding and exhausting. I often wondered if the painful process would be worthwhile in the end, and on the other side, I can tell you it was. I'm thankful Catherine continued to encourage me to show up. She knew it was going to be hard work, and she didn't sugarcoat it; I left each session with a list of action steps to work on during the week. These tasks required me to process what we'd worked on instead of numbing out with my default mode of busyness.

To process the thought patterns I'd become accustomed to, I had to take an honest look at my life. I had to take off the mask and stop pretending I was fine. Because I didn't want to be fine anymore; I wanted *fantastic*. And to get there, to do any real healing, I needed to show up and receive the help that was being offered to me. I needed to painstakingly go back to the same limiting beliefs over and over again.

My internal programming was to believe that I was responsible for taking care of myself and couldn't lean on anyone. This belief had crept into every crevice of my life, and let me tell you, weeding it out was *work*. I know I'm not alone in needing to learn the same lessons repeatedly over the course of life. Each time a variation of the same lie I had been telling myself for years crept in, Catherine had the patience to point back to where it originated. She illuminated the lie that was festering in my soul and stepped in with vibrant and anchoring truth. Slowly but surely, I learned I could lean on others, that everything wasn't my sole burden to carry. It was like breathing fresh air for the first time.

Role Reversal

I've had the privilege of being the mentor who helps weed out lies and pulls out the gold as well. A former Young Life gal of mine, who over the ten years of our friendship had become something between a sister and a friend, started going down the rabbit hole of self-analysis. Through listening to her processing, I realized that somewhere along the way she'd lost the belief that she was extraordinary. Don't we all do this?

It was in that moment that I leaned in and told her I was completely invested in her process of self-discovery. I reminded her that she was free to question her beliefs and put it all on the table. But I said one thing I would not stand for was her selling herself short.

As my role began to reverse, from being championed to championing, I made it clear that the one time I would override the direction the conversation was going was when she started letting that inner critic deceive her. I told her I would stand in the gap and remind her time and time again of exactly who she is—an extraordinary daughter of God.

It was easy for me to see her golden qualities she was having a hard time seeing on her own. Don't we all need someone to do this for us from time to time? I know that without the women in my life standing in the gap, fighting for me to become the best version of myself, I would not be the woman I am today. They kept me from being swindled into believing the lies the Enemy tries to con us into. And because of that, I'm committed to empowering the women coming behind me and replacing the lies they've believed with truth.

Because I was shown this type of love, I now can offer the same.

—— Questions for Discussion and Reflection ——

1. Who has come into your life at just the right time?
   How so?

2. Have you ever felt like you showed up for someone at
   just the right time? How so?

3. How can you foster a spirit of vulnerability and
   humility in your daily life, starting today?

4. When you need to be taken off the rabbit trail of
   negative self-talk and limiting beliefs, how can
   someone best help you?

·····

Action Step: This week, get intentional about noticing your
thought patterns. When you're tempted to numb out, think
about what feeling, conversation, or painful memory you
might be trying to avoid. Then take steps to face it.

MENTORS PROPEL
YOU FORWARD

NINE

Anne

A year and a half into my time in Colorado, before Catherine and I had done much of our work together, I had grown my online business to a place where I could match my salary and quit my day job. But I was running hard in a million different directions. I was managing Instagram accounts for clients, launching an online magazine, stewarding a tribe of women to write for the magazine—and drowning all the while.

When I first started running my own business, I was utterly clueless. I had no road map for what I was doing, and I was swinging on a pendulum between being utterly terrified at needing to make a profit and the sheer excitement of all the possibilities. Some days I vacillated from imagining myself penniless and living in my parents' guest bedroom to dreaming of driving down the road in my future Mercedes G-Wagen.

I had no idea how to manage the growth and expansion of my budding Instagram agency, my portfolio of eCourses, and my

Dream to Done coaching program. My business kept demanding more and more, and I soon realized that it might be beneficial for me to find some type of business mentor—someone who could understand the nuances of running an online business and had expertise in this field.

Right around this time, an email rolled into my in-box. It was from Anne. I'd first encountered her work a few years before on an online training course I was taking, where she spoke about developing a unique message. I hopped on her email list, and now she was offering people the opportunity to join a new program she was launching.

This was an opportunity to work closely with her as a beta tester for one of her upcoming programs, and I had the odd sensation that if I applied, I'd get it. Now, let me be clear: I am not the girl who's always winning contests and giveaways. I had no reason to believe that I would be chosen out of what I assumed would be hundreds of applications. I simply felt a certainty that, if I applied, Anne and I would work together.

What was there to lose? I quickly made a video with my laptop and sent it off for Anne to be the judge of whether I made the cut. Lo and behold, I did. And a few months later, the doors opened, and our journey together began.

Soldiering On

When I joined Anne's business mastermind, I was given a safe space to bounce around ideas, seek counsel, and hone my craft with the help of someone who had gone before me. I was beyond excited to have personal feedback from a woman I had deeply admired in the online business space. She's an entrepreneurial magician, and in my mind nothing was greater than to have her personal input in my career.

For the two years prior, I had been building my business and crushing one goal after another. I'm a doer by nature, so with a little guidance, I was ready and eager to take on the world. Nothing could hold me back—except maybe exhaustion.

I met Anne with big dreams in my heart and an extremely full plate. I was running full steam ahead with my various projects and to say I was stretched thin would be an understatement.

Yet, per usual, I *pushed through*. I was juggling way too many hats, and I was at the point where my clients and audience were getting the very best of me while my friends and family were getting the absolute worst. I knew I needed to rest, to take a break, but I just didn't know how. I thought, *Sure, I could use some rest. Maybe just a weekend off. But do breaks even exist when you're running your own business?* I knew I'd get around to it one day. Maybe if I worked hard enough, I could be like those people running their businesses from under a palm tree on the beach. That laptop lifestyle (which I now know is an illusion) wasn't quite yet in sight for me, but I thought if I worked hard enough, I could make it happen.

Most weeks my working hours stretched into 12-hour days. Today, I laugh as I listen to my first podcast episode, where another young entrepreneur and I both commented that our work days normally wound down about 10 p.m. We thought this was normal! Each day was jam-packed with six to eight lengthy calls introducing myself and my business to new clients, not to mention the actual workload between conversations. My stress wasn't surfacing in an easily recognizable way but rather in irritable outbursts and a type of body ache that had me thinking my spine was out of alignment. I hurt all over, every single day. But like a good soldier, I kept trudging on.

As it turned out, what was true of my personal life was also true of my business. As Catherine, my therapist, helped me uproot deeply embedded lies and replace them with truth, I needed help learning how to walk out those principles not just in my day-to-day life but specifically in my career.

In that season of burning my business candle at both ends, Anne recognized that my pace wasn't sustainable and that soon I wouldn't have the energy to continue.

Going Slow

What drew me to Anne in the first place was that I felt safe with her, like I could lay down all pretenses. In a career field where everyone puts on her best face and avoids showing vulnerability, I needed someone who had navigated my industry and managed to stay true to herself. I needed help setting a pace that was manageable in an ever-changing landscape. And thankfully, with Anne, I hit the jackpot.

As my first career-focused mentor, Anne cultivated a totally open, judgment-free environment to wade through the waters of burnout and come out on the other side. With her, I felt free from all the expectations I had taken on—not just from others but from myself. I didn't need to keep growing and meeting new milestones every month. I didn't need to sprint through what was supposed to be a marathon! Anne allowed me to shortcut all the marketing tactics that promised instant success overnight when she reminded me there's no instant success in *any* business.

Under her care, and through trial and error, I discovered my capacity and settled on realistic limits for my workload, allowing my business to operate in a way that let me thrive personally. I was able to slow down and rebuild my career at a healthy, sustainable pace. Along the way, she helped me gauge the best use of my time and discern when my activity was unproductive. I saw from her example that one can be successful *and* go slow, intentionally stepping back from the pace that causes so many to become bitter and burned out.

Anne had three incredible qualities that set her apart as a mentor:

- *She made me do the work.* Anne never gave me an exact road map. Instead, she offered herself as a sounding board to help me gain understanding for what could be next. Those are the best teachers—the ones who give you the space to figure things out.

- *She was patient.* I watched Anne take time to learn about changes in her industry and study how they might play out long-term instead of rushing to implement all the shiny new tactics or strategies that came her way—probably the perks of being in her industry for more than ten years and seeing trends come and go.

- *She believed I could do it.* Anne believed in linking arms with others and doing what she could with what she knew to propel them into their dreams. Because she believed in me, I was able to rest, recover, and get back up stronger and more equipped, then move forward in my business with more gusto and tenacity than ever before, taking it to the next level without sacrificing my sanity.

Linking Arms

Anne was everything I didn't know I needed in a business mentor. So many women get caught up in the rat race when it comes to their careers. In a world that says *more, faster, better, now,* Anne was a breath of fresh air, pouring into others when most people were withholding what they could have offered. Rather than adopting the mind-set of competition that seems to run rampant with women in business, she generously offered me best practices she'd learned. In doing so, she enabled me to work effectively from a place of rest rather than a place of constantly striving.

Until I was neck deep in my industry, I had no idea how rare finding someone like Anne was. We see the phrase "collaboration over competition" plastered across co-working spaces and office walls, but even in those environments the phrase is often preached but not practiced. Anne was living proof that there really are women who live out this message. She showed me that only through linking arms can we achieve the impact we hope for. If we're going to leave a mark on this world, we have to lay down the old tactics of competitiveness; the only way we can steward our dreams to break through our own glass ceiling is through partnership. Competition will never get us there. If we're going to finish this race, it will be because we carried one another.

> The only way we can steward our dreams and break through our own glass ceiling is through partnership. Competition will never get us there.

Rhythms of Rest

I remember when I was coming out of burnout. We were inching closer to Christmas, and by stripping my business down to the bare bones and prioritizing only what was necessary, I had some newfound space in my day. And by "space" I mean I was now working 40-hour weeks instead of 70- to 80-hour weeks. But I was bored with this newfound time. I had no idea how to run at a slower, healthier pace that would set me up for longevity in my business, not burnout.

I found myself daydreaming about getting a little part-time gig at Anthropologie. It would be *so fun* and "just for the holidays," I promised myself. Thankfully, a friend slapped me upside the head with a heavy dose of reality and practically screamed at me, "You're supposed to be resting!" I ended up not applying for the job, and I slowly but surely slipped into new rhythms, finding actual hobbies outside of work to fill my time.

It wasn't long before I could share the same wisdom Anne had given me with a longtime mentee and friend. During the next holiday season, this sister-friend came to me for business advice. At this point, she was juggling three full-time businesses. Not one, *three*. And she said to me, "I'm a little bored. I think I'm going to get a part-time job at Anthropologie for fun."

Face-palm, y'all.

I lovingly said, "No way!" I told her how finding my own rhythms of rest often felt like living in a prison of boredom, but it was slowly getting better. And it did for her too.

We absolutely need one another to reach the heights of success and impact we all hope for. Instead of idly watching from the sidelines as someone makes mistakes that could hold them back for years to come, we can step in and offer them the result of our experiences for them to learn from.

A mentor who can sit back and offer a different perspective might just be the piece of the puzzle that propels us forward in our career. My mentors have often been able to see possibilities for my life and the directions my path might take, and I have been able to turn around and offer the same gift to those who came behind me.

—— Questions for Discussion and Reflection ——

1. Have you ever experienced burnout? What caused it?

2. Who do you most admire in your industry? Whose career path do you most admire? How might you reach out to that person?

3. Is there anyone in your career field you could mentor?

4. What has your experience been like with other women in the workplace? In what ways have you sensed competition?

• • • • •

Action Step: This week, consider the pace of your work. If you're running too fast, susceptible to burnout, ask trusted mentors for advice about how you can adopt a pace that's more sustainable.

MENTORS INVEST GENEROUSLY

TEN

Amber

met Amber because of a Facebook ad, and what attracted me to her was her warm spirit. In real life, she seemed like my kind of gal, like many of the mentors you've already read about who sat across the table from me in coffee shops.

But with Amber, mentorship would be in the context of a paid coaching program, and at this point I had never invested in paid mentorship. She and I also had no previous connections. But something in my spirit said working with her was a smart choice for me. And as I went beyond that gut feeling and did due diligence in researching her background, I found her to have quite a track record in business, having consulted both small businesses and larger corporations.

This would be a huge step toward expanding and scaling my business in a way I couldn't do on my own. I was two years into running my business and had just started working with Anne, and I needed all the guidance I could get. But when the opportunity to work with Amber came up, I had never invested more than a few hundred dollars in my business at a time. The fact that her coaching would cost a few thousand dollars made me hesitate.

Again, it just felt right. So I pulled the trigger before even talking to my husband (*not recommended*). Maybe that wasn't my finest moment, but that $200 a month that felt so big at the time became one of the most worthwhile investments I have ever made.

Up to this point, *so* many women had stepped into the role of mentor and shared everything they knew with me. But when it came to a voice of guidance in my business, I needed to level up and ask for help with strategy. There comes a time when picking people's brains goes only so far in your career. And while it's natural to start off gleaning everything there is to know from friends, family, and even loose connections who may be willing to sit down with coffee and spill the beans about your industry, at some point a coffee date will no longer suffice. You need a formal mentor.

> **There comes a time when picking people's brains goes only so far in your career.**

It's not that coffee dates aren't great, but sometimes you just need more organized input. If you're building a dream or a business, pick-your-brain coffee dates will no longer provide the structure or value sufficient for where you need to go. When it comes to gleaning from someone's knowledge that goes beyond life experience and into business strategy, it's totally appropriate to invest monetarily in that mentoring relationship.

Pick Your People

If I was going to invest, I wanted to invest in the best. Amber had studied in Johns Hopkins' MBA program, served as a business consultant for corporate companies, and built a group coaching program that would go on to serve as the model for my own. She was an accomplished woman who, through her coaching services, offered me a shortcut to learning the same strategies she'd invested years to learn.

I also loved that while Amber worked with the best of the best, she was still warm and relatable, never cutthroat or pretentious. She was available to her more than 100 clients in the most open way I had seen modeled, but she also had strong enough boundaries to avoid wearing herself out or making her family feel neglected for the sake of her business. She showed me that I, too, could show up with warmth and openness, which I'd not often seen modeled in the business world.

For me, Amber was a breath of fresh air because, as I looked around, I saw a stark pendulum swinging between "maverick" style business coaches and "feel-good" style life coaches. I needed someone right in the middle—equal parts strategy and lifestyle.

The business world operates on the principle of attracting and repelling. When you're asking people to pay you for a service, your goal is to attract the people who will get the most out of your service and discourage those who aren't a good fit. Amber attracted me because I could tell I'd benefit most by being in her sphere of influence.

As a mentor in business myself, I try to keep this dynamic in mind. It's my job to communicate how I can help people and to remember that I can't help *all* people. Not everyone who stumbles across my website and social feeds will benefit from my support. Sometimes I need to communicate that they would be better served by another mentor, someone who can share exactly what they need.

These instances—when I'm not the right fit to mentor someone—

provide me with an opportunity to lift up another fellow entrepreneur sister. If you know you're not the best person to mentor a specific person, instead of trying to force the relationship and attempting to be something for them you're not, steer them toward someone you know would suit and serve them better. We will all go so much further in this space when we learn to support one another's giftings!

The Relational Side

Choosing and paying for a mentor can be scary, and I think our aversion to it comes from the fear of being swindled within the context of a role that is also highly relational. But when you're paying a mentor, they're often paying someone else to invest in them too. This results in a trickle-down effect of information that enables us to truly link arms to propel one another forward.

Working with a paid mentor means you have access to someone who can coach you when problems arise. Not everyone will drop what they're doing or be equipped to give valuable input when crises occur. But by working with someone in a paid context, you have expectations within the parameters the mentor sets up. Because Amber set up the parameter that it's appropriate for me to reach out to her at any point something unexpected arises in my business, I can text her and get feedback within a few days. Of course, I don't take that lightly—I am extra careful with boundaries, never overwhelming her—or any of my mentors—with the need for constant attention, and I always have a heart to give back.

Having friends and family around to give advice on business and career is great, but their advice can take you only so far. Unlike a family member or a friend, a paid mentor lays out all the expectations in the relationship so you'll know what they will do for you and how they'll show up. When it comes to running a business, you need someone to come alongside you for the big wins and also help you pick up the pieces when everything falls apart.

It's important to respect and honor the mentors in your life and appreciate the value of all they're pouring into you. Paying them for their expertise—especially in business—is a way to honor the time, years of world experience, and personal monetary investment they pour into the wisdom they're now passing along. In a professional mentorship there are different sets of expectations and boundaries, and those can be a blessing because they never muddy the waters of the type of relationship you have.

I attribute much of the success I've had in my career to Amber and Anne, the two mentors who walked with me through this entrepreneurial journey every step of the way. I often say they're stuck with me for life. And I say this lovingly because, in our day and age, the messaging around getting ahead in our careers is to glean everything possible from someone and then move on to the next "networking" opportunity. This idea runs rampant, but there is a better way.

You don't need the shiniest new person in your industry. You don't need the latest and greatest by the crowd's standards. You don't need the person to have a gazillion Instagram followers or a blue check mark beside their name. You simply need someone *willing* to invest in you. Willingness is what makes a mentor great.

By choosing Amber as my first formal paid mentor, I won the lottery. Her generosity showed me how I want to champion other women I mentor.

Amber was not only there for me as I built my business but also as I rebuilt it. She was there the day my worst fear came true—one algorithm change flipped my six-figure business upside down. She was there in the aftermath as I wondered if I had hit my peak at age 29 and it was all downhill from there. She encouraged me every step of the way and reminded me that I hadn't hit my peak—I was just getting started. She was there as I weighed the odds of rebuilding or going back to a day job. She was there through the messy parts and chose to make an investment in me that was above and beyond anything I could have asked of her.

> People who ask for help when everything is okay are much more likely to not just survive a hard season but thrive.

I'm so glad I sought Amber's wisdom and input into my life and business during the mountaintop moments, because she was there for the biggest valley I had faced in my career to date. Statistically speaking, people who ask for help when everything is okay are much more likely to not just survive a hard season but thrive. Maybe someone will be willing to step in during a hard season, but wouldn't it be more helpful if you had asked them to come alongside you when all was well? If I hadn't believed enough in the process to invest in a business mentorship when everything was peachy, I wouldn't have had Amber and all our relational history built up when I was most in need.

It Starts with Service

You can't magically have the mentor of your dreams without being willing to invest your time, your energy, and, yes, sometimes your money too. If you want a mentor, you need to show up. Maybe that means financially showing up and making the leap to invest in a paid mentor. Maybe that means not flaking out on coffee dates. Maybe that means investing in your mentor instead of just using your time together to unload all your problems.

Mentorship is a two-way relationship, and it starts with you. Amber didn't magically find me on the Internet and appear in my life with an offer to sweep me off my feet in the mentorship department. Quite the opposite—I invested in her program. I showed up. I offered thoughtful feedback to the group. I was just another person out of a hundred people who signed up for that group, but I set myself apart by offering to serve her in any way that might be helpful. I didn't make it just about me; I made the relationship mutual.

The success I've experienced with women investing so generously in me has happened because I showed up too. I didn't just show up to just receive but also to give.

As a mentor myself, the people I love investing in most are those who ask me about my life. There's a stark difference between the depth of relationship with people who merely seek to receive in our interactions and those who help to cultivate a more reciprocal dynamic.

When I'm in the paid role, I show up to every call expecting to be the one doing most of the giving. But when someone takes five minutes to ask me about my day and I let that person in a little bit more, the relationship dynamic changes subtly. With each subtle change, you can create mutually beneficial, open-handed relationships with both the mentors and mentees in your life—a change sure to be rewarding.

Here's an example: My number-one red flag is receiving an email or message that starts, "Can I pick your brain?" Now, those in my circle—whether they're friends or those I mentor—have full access to my brain. They can ask me anything, and I will share everything I know because we have a relationship. But when a stranger reaches out, out of the blue, and asks to pick my brain, I say, *Thank you, next!*

Why does this bother me so much? Beyond the fact that *Can I pick your brain?* is a phrase I find a tad bit annoying, I get that request weekly, and it's not coming from a desire to build any kind of relationship with me. It's coming from a place of *What can you give me?*

I can guarantee that most of the women you look up to in your field experience the same thing. Their in-boxes are no doubt full of emails from people asking for things and requesting advice. So how can you stand out to them? And how can you level up your business game at the same time?

By serving. By seeking to bless and support the people you'd like to help support you.

> As you consider your relationships, especially the people from whom you want to learn, ask yourself if you're willing to be generous.

Now, don't get me wrong. I don't give in order to get. I give my time without expecting anything in return. I genuinely love making friends with every person I come into contact with, not thinking about what they can do for me but how I can show up and serve them. So as you consider your relationships, especially the people from whom you want to learn, ask yourself if you're willing to be generous. Think about ways you could use your time, wisdom, and resources to give back to the person who will so generously invest in you. And then when it's your turn to be the mentor, let's all take a note from Amber's book and give just as generously.

Ditching Transactional Relationships

I believe an ideal mentoring relationship comes down to two things: allowing it to develop over time and pulling the plug if there is even a hint that it feels transactional.

Let's start with allowing a relationship to develop over time. My relationships with my mentors didn't begin with us glued at the hip. Like any other participant in their mentoring programs, I hopped on the calls each week, I participated, and I contributed thoughtful feedback and ideas—not only to my mentors but to the other people in the group. I was one of many participants, and I didn't have anything special that made me stand out from the group to get noticed. I simply showed up. I was ready to invest more than just my time because I valued these women's investment in my life so much.

My relationships with both Amber and Anne did indeed progress over time, and we mutually grew to love and appreciate one another. I think a lot of that came down to my commitment to showing up to serve, not just take. I've found this to be instrumental in building deep mentoring relationships that turn into friendships—and even beyond, into relationships that feel like family.

The reality is that, as a mentor, there's so much fear about people sucking you dry because of the constant "give," and so many mentees don't think to give back. So as a mentee, think about how you can give back and support your mentor as they support you. Investing right back into the women who are investing in you—in a healthy and respectful way—will help you stand out in any circle.

My mentoring experiences are not the norm; I will own that. But I haven't approached them like so many people do. Even in

> Learning from women ahead of me is fun. But building friendships that last a lifetime is even better.

cases when I was paying for a mentorship program, I looked for opportunities to serve my mentor—not in an overbearing way, but through communicating I was happy to use my gifts and talents to benefit her goals as she simultaneously helped me to reach mine. Learning from women ahead of me is fun. But building friendships that last a lifetime is even better.

You know the phrase *It's lonely at the top?* Have you ever thought that the person you're looking up to may be yearning to be "known" in the same way you are? Take the time to get to know your mentor. Ask about her life. Check in on her when you know something big is going on. You might just be met with an openness and connectedness you never expected. As excited as you are to have someone pour into and invest in your life, I'm almost certain your mentors are looking for others to pour into them as well.

Heart to Swap

Finding the right mentor is just as much a trial-and-error process as is any other relational search, and sometimes a relationship turns out to be not a great fit. One indicator of that is when a relationship becomes transactional.

When I say *transactional,* I don't simply mean money or services being exchanged. I'm talking about a gut feeling or intuition that your interactions are all about what you can get from someone or what they can get from you instead of how you can mutually help each other.

In most situations in my life, finding a mentor hasn't been quick. But once I knew I'd found the right person, it was easy to build true connectedness and a relationship where we could both share knowledge with the other. While I might be gleaning from them how to steward and scale my business for long-term success, for instance, they might be learning the newest scrappy marketing strategy from me!

I call this the heart-to-swap strategy, and it has served me well. I've found that when people are approached with a heart to serve, they're quick to invest in that person who doesn't just want to "take" from the relationship. But sometimes my heart-to-swap style of serving has backfired. I've had the unlucky experience of working with a mentor who wanted only what I offered. Her "mentorship" of me was more of an afterthought.

Sometimes we run into someone we *think* we want as a mentor, only to find they may have only ever experienced this "taking" style of relationship. The idea of "What can I get out of someone else to further my career or ambitions?" isn't always stated in such an obvious way of operating, but it does run rampant in both ministry and business spaces.

You won't make it through life without stumbling into relationships that are more transactional in nature. And that's unfortunate, because we're in a day and age when women are supposed to be linking arms to propel one another forward. That *is* happening, but as much as we're moving forward, we don't always get it right, and we're simply bound to run into transactional relationships on occasion.

Here's the thing, though: We can still learn from these situations.

Asking anyone to be a mentor is a risk. Until you dive into a relationship with someone, you don't really know if the public persona they project is the same as who they are inside. Sometimes you get into the swing of a mentoring relationship only to realize the other person may not have had the same approach in mind you did.

Listen to your intuition when it comes to finding the right type of mentor. My heart to serve my mentors has benefited me, but with this approach comes the risk that someone might say yes only because of something you can offer her. Even though my approach opens the door for a bit of pain, taking this risk is better than not serving at all. When someone is investing so much in me, it's only natural for me to want to give back.

In these cases, it will be important to be in tune with your internal caution lights and set up some boundaries. If you start to feel like your mentor is using you—or if you realize you're using the person in front of you—politely end the relationship. It's challenging to do this, but it's better than each of you continuing to show up to the table stretched thin and bitter because neither of you is setting or observing healthy boundaries.

Again, I'm a big believer in the heart-to-swap strategy, so I'd strongly recommend offering up a skill set that might be beneficial to a potential mentor in exchange for their time. For example, I'm skilled at digital marketing, and I can serve my mentors with those abilities in their own businesses or ministries.

Maybe, though, you're looking to be mentored and don't feel you have anything to offer. But you can serve mentors in many ways! Here are a few possibilities:

- If they offer a service, refer people to them when you hear of someone who needs what they offer.

- Every once in a while, ask them if you can take anything off their plate that would make their life easier. Be prepared to do it.

- If they're hosting something like an event, conference, speaking engagement, or retreat, offer your support by volunteering to help, such as setting up or tearing down the venue.

- Be a good listener, and always seek opportunities to build them up and encourage them.

- Surprise them with a gift card to their favorite restaurant or store.

- If you're being mentored in business, you *will* eventually have a service, skill, or product. Offer it to them as a gift.

- Whenever you get together, offer to pay for the dinner or drinks.

- And don't forget to say thank you! Simply acknowledging and telling your mentor what their guidance means to you will make a huge impact.

In most cases, swapping from the heart has worked well for me and for the mentoring women I've approached with this offer. I'm always trying to create a dynamic where reciprocity is key—a mutual understanding that both parties in the relationship are in it to offer their wisdom with radical openhandedness, to show up, and to share what they know with each other, blurring the lines between mentor and mentee.

The crux of true connectedness is found in serving, not in taking. And it's Jesus who stands as our model of servant leadership. He regularly sought to bless the people He surrounded Himself with and was never above humbling Himself to honor others. As we look to Him as our model, we are better able to love and serve one another in our businesses and relationships.

—— Questions for Discussion and Reflection ——

1. What is one way you can give generously today?

2. Who in your life exemplifies generosity?

3. Think about your ideal mentor. What is your strategy for reaching out to someone like that?

4. How do you think having a paid mentor could benefit you in your business journey?

5. What are the giftings you have to share with others/serve others with?

· · · · ·

Action Step: This week, cultivate a "heart to swap." Brainstorm a way you can show up to serve someone in your life, putting the relationship before your own needs.

Learning While Leading

The ten women featured in this book have been some of the greatest influences in my life to date, but they are not and will not be my only mentors. I have mentors in friendship, mentors in business, mentors in marriage, and I hope in the future I'll have mentors in parenthood.

None of the mentors I've had made an impact on my life because they were perfect or had everything figured out. Instead they taught me the value of support, consistency, and accountability. They showed vulnerability and a willingness to share what they learned in their own lives. And because of their investment in my life, I've sought to invest in women a few steps behind me, cheering them on as they wrestle with life, build their own business, and learn to love their family.

In my mentoring relationships, time and time again, I've seen that *mentors need mentors*. To be effective as leaders, we need to constantly strive to grow. Without emotional stability and agility, none of us have the tools to pour into the people God places in our lives. So as I try to be faithful with the influence I've been given, I continue to seek out advice and leadership from those who display the qualities I want to embody in hopes that I can pass that wisdom along to others down the road.

Mentors need mentors.

I had no idea what I was doing when I first started mentoring. But what 19-year-old does? My group of high school girls took me through the ringer. I walked with them through breakups and family heartbreak, and I walked with them through college when bigger issues arose, like deconstruction of faith, bouts of depression, and navigating the murky waters of growing up. What allowed us to keep it so real? Why did they trust me and let me in? The answer is simple: I didn't try to be anything I wasn't, and I certainly didn't ask them to do that either. This was one of those roles I learned on the job, but it set me up for a lifetime of humbly leading while learning.

I want to remind you that it's okay to consider mentoring even if you don't have it all figured out. Each of the women highlighted in this book taught me something about mentorship—and I hope they taught you something about it too. Did each of them excel in every department of life? No way. But they all showed up in a way that forever changed my perspective on the impact of mentorship.

If you're waiting for the day you're perfect to step up to the plate, you'll be waiting for the rest of your life. It's my hope that, after reading this book, you feel a bit more confident about looking at the women around you and choosing to learn from some of them. Even more so, it's my hope that you feel empowered to mentor others—because what we all learn at some point or another is that most of life is learning on the job.

My Aunt Michelle always says, "We start off in life like sandpaper. But I want the love of God to wear me down until I'm soft and smooth as velvet." Mentors can teach us how to be like velvet. They experience their own difficult seasons, learn and grow through them, and then willingly pass their wisdom down, allowing us to shortcut the distance through our own challenging experiences and go further than we ever imagined we could. And the most beautiful thing is it doesn't stop there: We get to turn around and do the same for others coming behind us.

Because we need each other. All of us.

ACKNOWLEDGMENTS

I n staying true to one of my favorite lines, *It takes a village*, it's only fitting that it took a village to bring this book to life.

To begin, I must honor the friends I invited into countless Google docs to review line after line, to make sure I stayed true to my vision for this book. Helping me bring this message to life was no easy task, and I'm forever grateful to the women who said "Yes!" when I called in the troops. Emily, Claire, Mary Cate, Meredith, Haley, Griffin, and Tiffany…I couldn't have done this without you.

To my husband, David—thank you for always being my number-one cheerleader. There is no one I'd rather have as my life partner and dream-mate. You make the world a better place, and your positive outlook on life and daily dad jokes keep me going.

To my gazillion parents—Mom, Dad, Nancy, Debbie, Dan, and Kevin—y'all are the best parents I could ask for. And to Grannie and Grandy—I love you to the moon and back.

To Kate—I can't believe we got to write books at the same time. Your constant support as you walked this path a few steps ahead of me made all the difference in my own journey. I am forever grateful for your companionship every step of the way.

To my agent, Tawny Johnson—thank you for being my advocate throughout this entire process and for making sure this book was brought to life in a way that felt 100 percent authentic. I struck gold with you!

To my team at Harvest House—I'm eternally grateful that you've walked hand in hand with me. Kathleen, I knew you were my girl the first time I heard your voice! I know I can be a lot to deal with, but I hope you enjoyed the ride as much as I did!

To those who wrote endorsements—thank you for believing in this message and for putting your name behind the idea that we women are better *together*. Every one of you has inspired the heart behind this book.

About the Author

Kelsey Chapman is an author, community builder, online educator, and host of *The Radiant Podcast*. She wholeheartedly believes dreams are worth pursuing, and she's passionate about teaching women how to walk with purpose in their gifts and live from a place of identity and rest—all so they can carry their dreams and vision for the long haul.

After a few years of fumbling her way through post-grad life and a brief stint overseas, Kelsey realized her entrepreneurial itch wasn't going away. She came home, got to work, and turned a part-time blog and side-hustle into a six-figure business in just two years. From there, she realized her business savvy traits and desire to empower others could be translated into something bigger through teaching everything she's learned with others. In just five years she has mentored hundreds of clients and thousands of students through building their brand, growing their platform, and stewarding their influence.

Today, Kelsey plays the role of personal cheerleader to an engaged audience of 100,000 followers, empowering and equipping women through her Dream To Done online mentorship program.

To learn more about Kelsey or to sign up for her newsletter, visit her at

www.kelseychapman.com
Instagram @kelschapman
Facebook @kelschapman
The Radiant Podcast
Available anywhere you listen to podcasts

To learn more about Harvest House books and
to read sample chapters, visit our website:

www.harvesthousepublishers.com

HARVEST HOUSE PUBLISHERS
EUGENE, OREGON